Exploring
Canework
in Polymer Clay

Color, Pattern, Surface Design

Exploring Canework
in Polymer Clay

Patricia Kimle

KALMBACH BOOKS

Kalmbach Books
21027 Crossroads Circle
Waukesha, Wisconsin 53186
www.Kalmbach.com/Books

Published in 2013
17 16 15 14 13   1 2 3 4 5

ISBN: 978-0-87116-450-6
EISBN: 978-0-87116-775-0

Editor: Karin Van Voorhees
Art Director: Lisa Bergman
Layout Designer: Lisa Schroeder
Photographer: William Zuback

Library of Congress Cataloging-in-Publication Data

Kimle, Patricia, 1967-
   Exploring canework in polymer clay : color, pattern, surface design / Patricia Kimle.

   p. : col. ill. ; cm.

   ISBN: 978-0-87116-450-6

   1. Polymer clay craft—Handbooks, manuals, etc. 2. Jewelry making—Handbooks, manuals, etc. 3. Costume jewelry—Handbooks, manuals, etc. I. Title.

TT297 .K56 2013
745.594/2

Contents

Introduction

It has been over 20 years since I opened my first package of polymer clay. In 1990 I was a fiber artist and a grad student living in a little apartment with little to no extra space for working in fiber. While taking a spinning class at a local yarn shop, I was introduced to polymer clay. Both the shop owner and I had read a magazine article about this new clay that could be used to make buttons and jewelry to match wearable art garments. Shortly after reading the article, the shop owner began to stock the clay, and of course, I had to try it. What began as a hobby that could fit in a shoebox eventually became my passion and allowed me to shape a career as an artist, professional designer, and teacher. I'm so glad you picked up this book and will allow me to introduce you to my love for polymer clay.

Polymer clay is one of the most versatile craft media available today. You can get started in polymer with just a few blocks of clay and minimal tools. A working kit can still fit in a shoebox, and it's a craft that can be adopted with a relatively small investment.

Polymer's applications are as varied as the artists who create with it. It is used for jewelry, home décor, scrapbooking and paper crafting, sculpting of character figurines, and fine art. Polymer clay can be worked in many techniques, including sculpting, painting, texturing, and, as you are about to explore, canework.

Patti Kimle

"Creativity is...seeing something that doesn't exist already. You need to find out how you can bring it into being and that way be a playmate with God."
– Michele Shea

GETTING STARTED

CANEWORK BASICS   An Early Innovation • Tools • Clay • Conditioning • Baking

DESIGN LESSONS   Color • Skinner Blend • Constructing and Reducing Canes • Cane Slices

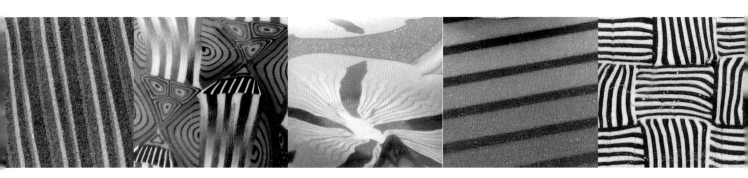

Polymer clay is synthetic modeling clay that remains malleable until it is baked. Chemically, it is a member of the plastics family; it is a PVC (polyvinyl chloride). Polymer clay comes in a wide variety of formulas and colors, which makes it accessible to creators of any age and ability. Artists have poetically described polymer as "three-dimensional color."

As with any type of art activity, a grounding in basic design principles allows one to be more purposeful and achieve more pleasing and successful projects. The elements and principles of design are the terms and concepts explored in most beginning design curricula no matter the art medium. In the following pages we will explore the elements of line, shape, color, scale, and pattern as they are especially relevant to the medium of polymer caning.

CANEWORK BASICS

An Early Innovation

Polymer clay was developed in the 1960s and 1970s as a craft product primarily for children. Colored clays were introduced in the 1970s, and artists began exploring the material for art and jewelry applications in the 1980s. By the early 1990s, clay was gaining popularity in the craft market and was fairly easy to find at retail.

The decade of the 1990s brought much innovation and experimentation in polymer techniques. First and foremost, techniques from other media were applied to polymer. The earliest and most prominent of these cross-over applications was a glasswork style alternately called Venetian glass, furnace glass, or millefiore: "many flowers" in Italian. In this technique, various colored glass rods are arranged and bundled to form flowers or geometric patterns. The bundle is heated in a furnace and stretched when the glass is molten hot. As it is stretched, the cylinder of glass is reduced in diameter, increased in length, and the pattern is reduced in scale while the arrangement of color and pattern remains intact. This process is also used with colored porcelain clays.

In polymer, the principle is the same: rolls, sheets, and shapes of clay are arranged in a larger loaf or log to form a cane. As the sides of the cane are compressed, it is reduced in dimension or diameter and increased in length. The fun part begins when a reduced cane is then cut up and recombined into another more detailed pattern. This process of reducing and recombining canes forms the basis for pattern design and is the ground we will explore in depth in later chapters.

Early pioneers in polymer canework include Pier Volkos, Steven Ford and David Forlano (known then as City Zen Cane), Martha Breen, Ruth Ann and Michael Grove, Kathleen Dustin, and many others. A wonderful resource featuring much of this early groundbreaking artwork is the website polymerartarchive.com.

Before we jump into cane making, let's review basic polymer clay tools and techniques.

Tools

The basic tool kit for canework is very simple. A sharp blade, an acrylic rod for rolling (I like to use both a 1-in. and a ¼-in. rod), and a needle tool are all you really need to get started. A pasta machine or clay roller allows for easy conditioning and the consistent rolling of clay into smooth sheets of varying thickness from about ⅛-in. thick to very thin.

Often, a cane will be cut up into equal pieces. It is convenient to work over a grid to make measuring and cutting easy. My work surface is a clear glass cutting board that is smooth on one side. Under it, I place a plastic sheet printed with an inch grid (found at fabric stores). There are also many kinds of printed cutting boards or plastic sheets available. Some of these are not compatible with clay, however, and either stick too much or absorb the clay oils and colors.

Canework is generally a "pure clay" technique. However, polymer clay is compatible with a wide variety of other art and craft media, including oil and acrylic paints, some inks, dry powder pigments and mica powders, rubber stamps, mixed media ephemera, and many others. Once you learn canework, it can be combined with textural elements and other techniques and media in composition.

As you explore jewelry making with polymer clay, you may add to your tool kit with shaped cutting tools, sculpting tools, and more—but for our purposes, these are the only tools you'll need for canework.

Clay

There are several widely available brands of polymer clay. Polyform Products produces the Sculpey family of clays, including Sculpey III, Premo Sculpey, and several special-use clays. KatoClay is made by VanAken Inc. Fimo, Fimo Soft, and Fimo Classic are produced by Eberhard Faber. Cernit is manufactured by The Clay Factory, Ltd. Pardo clay is a wax-based polymer clay manufactured by Viva Décor. These various brands are widely available in most U. S. craft chain stores or online. Search the Internet, as listings and suppliers change frequently.

Each brand and formula of clay has different working characteristics and finished properties. All the clays have a different consistency and working feel. Some are softer or stiffer direct from the package. I find it's a matter of personal preference, as each artist has a different hand temperature, different pressure in working with the clay, etc. In addition, all the clays have changed somewhat in the recent past as the companies have formulated clays that are phthalate-free. I recommend that you try one or two packages of each brand to identify the clay you prefer.

My personal choice for clay is Premo Sculpey. I like its working feel, and I love the color palette because it is based on artists' paint colors. All the projects in this book were made with Premo Sculpey.

Conditioning

Conditioning clay is the preparatory stage of kneading or rolling the clay into smooth sheets. Conditioning with a new package of clay will generally require only a few passes through the pasta machine to warm it up and create a smooth sheet. If the clay is old, it may take a bit more effort. If the clay is very firm and dry, there are additives that can aid in conditioning. Clay softener (an oil solvent) and liquid clay are available for most brands, especially for Sculpey brands, Kato, and Fimo.

All clays that will be combined in one cane should be fairly equal in consistency. If a cane is constructed with both soft clays and very firm clays, those clays will move differently during the reduction process, distorting the intended pattern and increasing the amount of waste to be trimmed from the ends of the cane. Achieve consistency through conditioning.

Baking

Polymer clay is a low-temperature curing medium, so it can be cured in a home oven, countertop oven, or toaster oven.

When the clay is heated, the PVC particles fuse together and the solvents evaporate. For most brands, the recommended curing temperature is 275°F. Always double-check the manufacturer's instructions on the package. Above 300°F, the clay can scorch or burn.

When the clay is overheated, light colors will darken excessively and, in extreme cases, the clay will emit noxious fumes. For this reason, keep an oven thermometer in the oven and preheat the oven. Insert the clay only when the oven has reached and is maintaining the appropriate temperature. It is always a good idea to dedicate an oven used to cure polymer clay to non-food use.

Finishing

After baking polymer clay, there is no further finishing step required. The plain "out of the oven" finish will differ by brand. Some brands have a matte finish and others have some sheen after baking. You can enhance the finish even further by sanding and buffing the surface, and/or applying a water-based gloss product.

Sand clay with wet-dry sandpaper and water. The water will control sanding dust, which shouldn't be inhaled; also, rinsing often prevents the sandpaper from clogging up with polymer particles. If a piece is fairly smooth and blemish-free to begin with, start sanding with 400-grit sandpaper. If there are nicks, bubbles, fingerprints, or other mistakes to remove, it may be necessary to use a coarser grit, such as 320 at first, to cut more quickly.

After smoothing the surface with 400, use finer grits for the finishing touches. It's up to you to determine how much to sand. I like to use 400, 600, and 800 grit and then polish.

Polishing

Polish polymer with a clean unstitched muslin wheel on a jeweler's lathe or a converted bench grinder or other rotary tool. Don't use rouge or polishing compound. Keep the clay object to be polished in the lower front quadrant of the wheel and hold it firmly, as the wheel can tend to grab the piece and send it flying. Always wear eye protection, and keep hair and loose clothing away from the wheel.

Hold the piece against the spinning muslin wheel lightly and keep it moving. Do not bear down hard or hold the piece still as this may result in the clay getting too hot and the fibers creating a burn mark on the surface. If this does happen, return to the sanding stage, remove the blemish, and polish again.

DESIGN LESSONS

Color

Color is perhaps the most important consideration in planning canework designs. Color choice should be determined not only by personal taste, but one must also consider the elements of value contrast, color harmonies, and the scale to which the intended pattern will be reduced.

The human eye can perceive millions of colors. Our perception and interpretation of color is a relative distinction. As children, we learn the various colors as they fall into broad categories. We learn the basic color names or color families. But eventually we learn that there is no "pure" color; we distinguish colors in relation to their properties relative to all possibilities. One picture that demonstrates these relative comparisons is the color wheel.

The basic color wheel is made up of the **primary colors** which are red, blue, and yellow. The result of mixing each of these color pairs are violet (or purple), green, and orange—the **secondary colors** (**A**). Then there are the **tertiary colors,** which are mixed from the pairings of each primary with its resulting secondary colors, giving us red-orange, red-violet, blue-green, and so on (**B**).

There are three basic properties of color: hue, saturation, and value. A **hue** is a specific, identifiable color. **Saturation** (also called intensity) is the purity of a color. **Value** is defined as the lightness or darkness of a color and is sometimes also called brightness. Let's examine each of these properties in a little more detail.

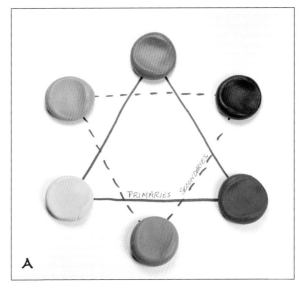

Primary and Secondary Colors

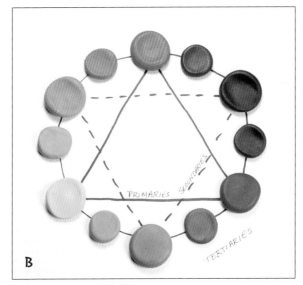

Tertiary or Intermediate Colors

C

Example of color temperature or bias.

Hue

Every color is perceived in relation to other colors around it. Every individual, specific color perceivable or imaginable is a hue. Our brain recognizes that a specific shade of green fits into the green category, but it also interprets that green in comparison to all the hues we have learned exist. This level of perception and distinction is learned, in that we share references from nature and culture in the naming of colors. Some examples of nature references include green tomato, lime green, spruce green, or avocado. Cultural names include fire engine red, flag red, or barn red. Yet even though this knowledge is shared, we each interpret color individually.

If I were to ask a dozen students to take a set of paints or polymer clay colors and mix an avocado green or a barn red, they would produce 12 separate hues of green and 12 of red. Most would appear very similar, but no two would be exactly alike in all three of color's basic properties of hue, value, and saturation.

Identifying a hue becomes the challenge solved by various color systems. In the print color system, primary colors are cyan, magenta, and yellow (CMYK; the K is black). Every color can be identified as a percentage of CMYK inks. Similarly, video screen colors can be identified in different photo/art software packages. For instance, Photoshop Elements includes the notation of percentages in the RBG (red, blue, green) color system, HSB (hue position, percentage of saturation, and brightness), or a color's numerical position in the hexadecimal system.

In polymer clay, every brand has a different color palette of packaged colors. Additionally, some brands have several colors that can serve as primaries for mixing. These colors vary relative to their color temperature, sometimes called bias. These four reds in the photo (C) vary in warmth or bias toward their neighboring colors of orange or violet.

Artists must identify the set of primary colors that will yield the most pleasing overall color palette according to personal taste. Additionally, because of the nature of the pigments used for clays, some primaries will yield purer or clearer secondary or tertiary colors.

When I teach color theory for polymer clay, I ask students to mix colors using the Skinner blend (p. 18) so they can quickly see the shifting of color proportionally across a blend. Marking the proportions of the blend allows one to quickly identify a formula for color mixing. This photo (D) demonstrates the possible variations using three of the Premo reds to explore color mixing and identify a favorite red for future use.

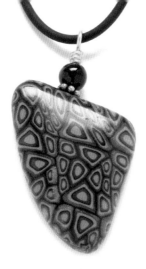

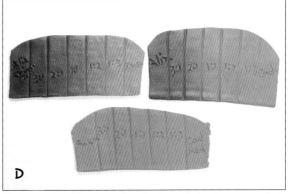

D

Mix colors in a blend to select the best choice for your project.

Saturation

What we think of as pure primary or secondary hues from basic color families are highly saturated colors. Less saturated colors have other colors mixed into them. When a color is mixed with some of its complement (the color appearing directly opposite on the color wheel,) it becomes less saturated. When all three primary colors are mixed, the result is the neutral colors (E).

A complementary pair includes a primary and a secondary color. Since the secondary includes the other two primaries, a complementary mix will therefore include some proportion of all three primaries. The pure neutrals include grays, ochres, and russets.

When you blend scrap clay from a project, often a neutral is produced. If it is not a clear, pure color relationship, it may yield what clayers commonly call mud. However, mud is often useful as a blending clay when you simply want to reduce the purity of a color slightly.

Value

The readability of color and pattern in a cane depends on the level of value contrast between adjacent colors in a pattern. A high level of contrast allows a cane pattern to be reduced to a smaller scale and still be readable. This becomes more important when a pattern is reduced and repeated multiple times (F).

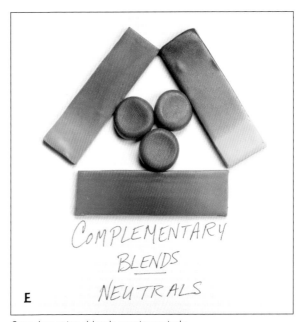

E

Complementary blends create neutrals.

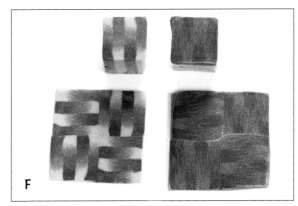

F

Color contrast aids readability.

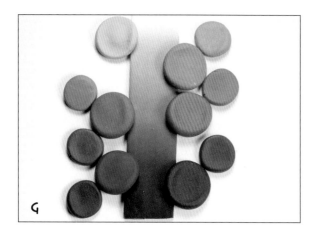

G

H

+ ⌣ = TINT

+ • = TONE

+ ◦ = SHADE

I

J

K

Every pure color on the color wheel has an initial value. For instance, pure yellow is a higher value than blue or purple (**G**).

Ensuring value contrast is important even in pure colors. Note that the hues of red and green are very similar in position on the value scale. Early in my caning experience, I learned that the classic Christmas-color cane may not be readable when the pattern is reduced to a smaller scale. Because there is very little value contrast, the two colors quickly begin to optically blend and appear as a brown color to the eye (**H**).

Value in mixed colors is influenced by saturation. When a color is mixed with its complement and its saturation is lowered, its value also is lowered. Color value also is adjusted by mixing with white, gray, or black. A **tint** is a color mixed with white. A **tone** is a color mixed with gray. A **shade** is a color mixed with black (**I**).

The value contrast used in a project influences the character of the project. Higher contrast designs, especially those including black and white, convey a more graphic feeling, whereas the same cane design appears more naturalistic or organic with less value contrast (**J**).

Color Schemes

A color palette is a finite, selected set of colors chosen for a perceived harmonious relationship for a particular design process. Color palettes are subjective and personal. Color palettes can be inspired by many things, including another piece of artwork, nature, fabrics, or one's imagination (**K**).

Color schemes can also be chosen due to a systematic relationship among colors and their position on the color wheel. A **complementary** color scheme is one in which the two colors are directly across from each other on the color wheel. An **analogous** scheme is made up of two or three or four colors adjacent to each other on the color wheel. Analogous schemes must be managed carefully to ensure that there is enough value contrast for caning.

A **triad** scheme includes three colors that are equidistant from each other on the color wheel. The three primaries and the three secondaries are both triad schemes (**L**). More sophisticated schemes can be developed from tertiary colors. Even more important to remember, colors do not always have to be used at pure saturation. The color relationship can provide the basic relationship, but colors can be altered by reducing saturation by blending in a complement, or by using tints, tones, or shades (**M**).

Most brands of clay have some metallic or pearlized colors in the line that include powdered mica in the clay. The metallics and pearls add another layer of richness and shimmer to colors. They also have an influence on color mixing. I often mix at least a small proportion of metallic or pearl colors mixed into most of my color palettes.

In order to keep the purest color and lessen any unintended color influence, I often try to mix the nearest metallic shade into the base color. For example, I add pearl or silver to light colors and pastel tints. I add gold to warm colors such as reds and oranges. To brown and neutral colors, I add bronze or copper, and to enhance greens and blues, I add antique gold. Note that silver and pearl have very little opaque pigment in them, so they do not hold up well in caning when used without mixing a matte or opaque color with them (**N**).

NOTE

In the baking process, some color change can occur. Depending on the brand of clay and the color, the baked result may appear a shade or so darker than it appears in the raw clay. In most cases, this change is barely noticeable, but occasionally, it can be more significant, especially with some reds and blues.

If you want to match a fabric swatch or other color sample exactly, it is best to bake a sample of the colors to test the result. If colors darken more than desired, correct by adding 5–10% of white or another matte neutral, like ecru, to a color. A few minutes of experimenting is a good safeguard against building a cane in the wrong colors.

Triad Scheme

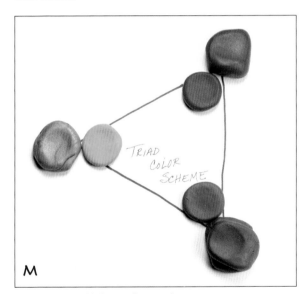

Triad scheme with lowered saturation

Pure metallic cane. Note the pearl tends to loose visual power when the cane is reduced.

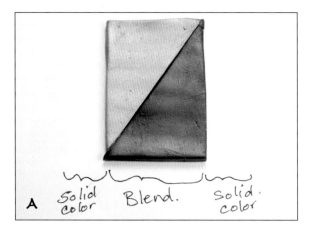

A Solid color   Blend.   Solid color

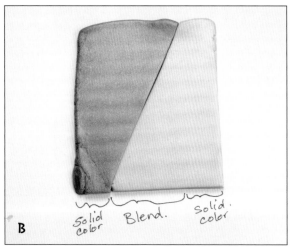

B Solid color   Blend.   Solid color

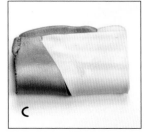

C

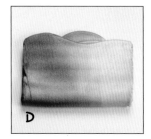

D

Skinner Blend

The Skinner blend is a technique for blending colors into sheets of graduated color. The Skinner blend is named for Judith Skinner, who first came up with the idea and shared it with the polymer community in the early 1990s.

A basic two-color blend begins with two right triangles arranged to form a rectangle. The diagonal cuts can go corner to corner (**A**) or can be inset some distance from the edge in order to preserve some of the original colors on each end (**B**).

After the colors are cut and arranged, fold the color sheet from bottom to top (**C**) and roll it through the pasta machine repeatedly. Always fold the clay sheet bottom to top, and always feed the clay into the pasta machine with the folded edge first into the rollers. Do not rotate the sheet. After four or five passes, the clay will begin to appear striped (**D**).

After 15 or 20 passes through the pasta machine, the stripes will disappear and the sheet will appear as a smooth gradation from one color to the other (**E**).

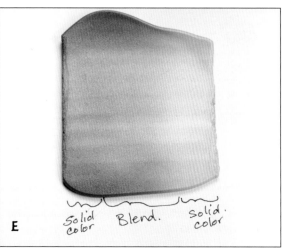

E Solid color   Blend.   Solid color

The Skinner blend will be a variation in many of the cane styles and projects to follow in this book. The blending of color softens the color contrasts and brings a degree of sophistication to the color palette. It also softens the hard, graphic nature of canework.

More than two colors can be blended into Skinner sheets. The arrangement of color must include triangular shapes that butt against each other and form a rectangle (**F**). The blending process is the same (**G**, **H**).

When the colors of your Skinner blend aren't quite right, you can remix the blend to influence the entire color range or just shift one side of a blend. To influence the entire blend, add color in whatever proportion is needed all the way across the blend (**I**). To influence only one side of the blend, add a triangular sheet of clay (**J**). Blend by folding and rolling as usual until the added color is completely mixed into the blend.

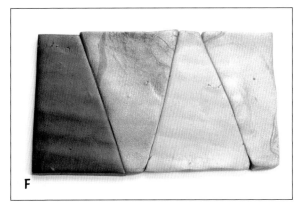

F

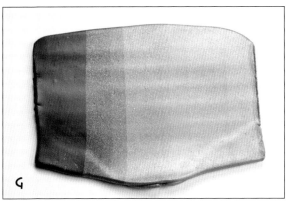

G

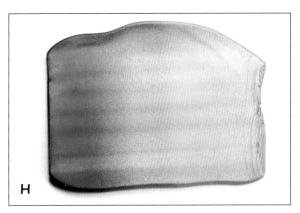

H

I

J

A

B

C

D

E

F

Constructing, Reducing, and Repeating

Constructing a cane is a process of arranging sheets and shapes of colors in three dimensions. The basic cane begins as a cylinder (log) or rectangular prism (brick or loaf) of clay. Make a pattern more complex by reducing a cane and repeating the element multiple times. Compressing the sides or diameter of the cane reduces its size in two dimensions and increases its length. If the cane is circular, the cane is rolled, squeezed, or stretched (**A**).

If it is a loaf or cube (**B**), the clay is pressed or pinched on the sides (**C**), and rolled occasionally along its length with an acrylic rod as it is stretched (**D**).

There will be a bit on each end where the pattern in the clay is distorted. This must be trimmed away before the cane is cut into pieces (**E**). The trimmed ends are scrap clay, which can be blended into a solid color, used as filler inside beads, or used as a backing sheet.

After the dimensions of the cane are reduced and lengthened, the cane can be cut into multiple pieces (**F**) and rearranged into a new cane with a more complex pattern. Depending on the pattern in the cane and the shape of the cane, the new cane can take one of several types of arrangements.

TIP✳

I keep a plastic bag on my studio counter for pieces of scrap clay. When I need inspiration, I blend chunks of this scrap clay and form a few bead core shapes. Usually, after a few beads, my muse kicks in with an idea or two.

Block Canes

In a block arrangement, square or rectangular canes are cut into even lengths and stacked in a regular pattern (**G**). Reduce the new cane again (**H**) and repeat the cutting and stacking (**I**). This process can be repeated until the scale of the pattern is at the desired size. However, at some point, a cane becomes "over-reduced;" the contrast is no longer readable and the colors appear blended.

Radial Canes

Canes can also be forced or pinched into different shapes. I like to form a cane into a triangular shape (**J**) and cut that triangle into two equal lengths. Then, I arrange the pieces against each other into a square with a mirror image on either side of the diagonal axis (**K**). Next, I reduce the cane again and cut it into four pieces to return it to a square cane, but rotate the cane units so that the original diagonal axes point to the center of the block. This is a radial arrangement (**L**).

This technique can also be used when an equilateral triangle cane is arranged into a hexagon, or the pattern can be reformed into a circle (**M**).

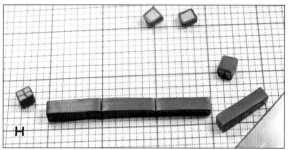

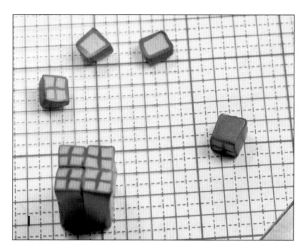

21

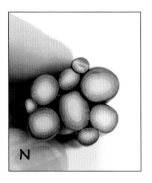

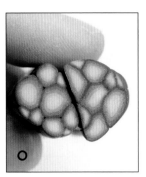

Random or Organic Canes

These occur when the cane elements are different shapes and sizes. For example, a round cane is reduced and cut into equal length pieces, but the diameters of the pieces differ (**N**). The pieces are assembled in a random arrangement and one must be careful not to press the resulting cane into a regular geometric shape if it is further reduced (**O**).

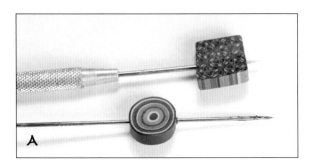

Cane Slices

There are many ways to use canes in jewelry. You can make beads, focal beads, pendants, pins, bracelets, and more. Cane slices can become beads when they are sliced about ¼-in. thick and pierced through (**A**).

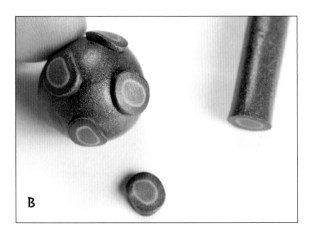

Canes can also be sliced very thin and applied to beads. The slices can be applied on the surface of a bead and left raised (**B**), or rolled into the background (**C**).

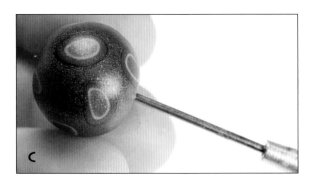

Use canes to cover the entire surface of a bead. I like to use scrap clay inside the bead (**D**). Roll the bead firmly to blend the seams. Use a thin rod to roll across and close the seams (**E**) before finishing by rolling the ball in the palm of your hand (**F**). This lessens the smearing of the pattern on the surface by the friction and the warmth of the hands.

Make patterned sheets of clay by laying out thin slices of canes onto a thin sheet of scrap clay as a backing layer. Roll the backing sheet about ¹⁄₁₆-in. thick, and slice the canes about that same thickness. Arrange the slices on the backing sheet. The slices can be arranged as elements floating on the background, or the slices can be arranged so that no background shows at all. Roll the cane slices into the background to blend them together without visible edges or seams, and so that the sheet is a consistent thickness (**G**).

Sheets of pattern can be used flat, wrapped over a form, or shaped against an armature. One attractive and lightweight bead style is called a lentil bead. Cut circles of clay and press them to a curved surface such as a burned out lightbulb (**H**). Bake while they are adhered to the glass. When cooled, glue the shaped halves together (**I**) and then apply additional clay (**J**) to accent the edge.

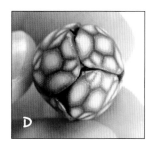
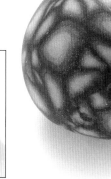
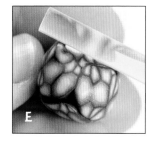

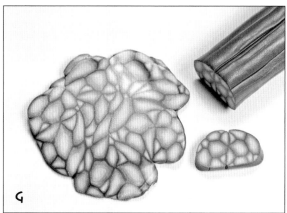
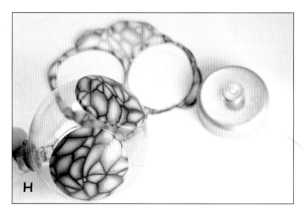

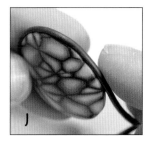
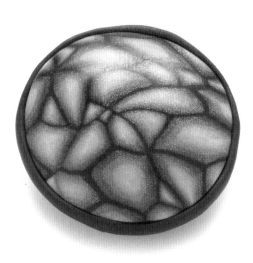

23

Block
Repeat

K

BRICK
REPEAT

L

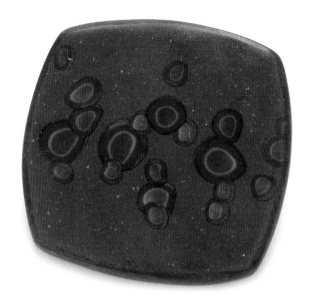

Use canes for larger **surface pattern**. Just as a cane element can be reduced and repeated to make a more complex patterned cane, slices of cane can be used to make sheets of pattern. Long ago, I studied fiber and surface design, and the lessons I learned about creating fabric pattern through surface design are just as applicable to polymer caning.

A **novelty pattern** is one where elements of design appear to float on a background. Novelty prints are usually subjective, suggesting a literal or figurative allusion. Novelty prints often are used in juvenile applications, like children's furnishings and apparel. In polymer, novelty patterns might include arrangements of floral canes, or other objects from reality.

Random or organic patterns are generally made of elements or design units in irregular shapes and sizes. Because there are not hard geometric lines and shapes or formal organization, the patterns tend to seem more natural and flowing.

In contrast, an **allover repeat pattern** is usually made from the arrangement of uniform geometric shapes. In a **block repeat**, a square or rectangular unit is arranged in rows **(K)**.

A **brick repeat** sets consecutive rows with units intersecting the midpoint of the previous row, just like bricks in a wall **(L)**.

A **half-drop repeat** is a brick repeat turned 90 degrees.

Since a polymer cane slice is a mirror image on front and back, there are many variations of allover repeats possible with the reversal or rotation of cane slices in a regular occurrence. **(M–O)**

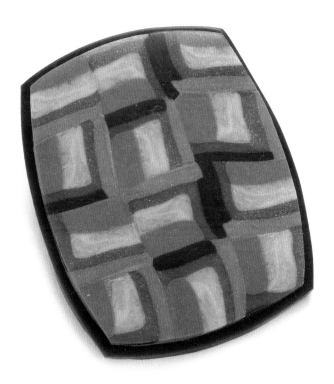

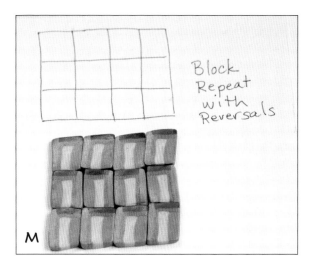

Block Repeat with Reversals

M

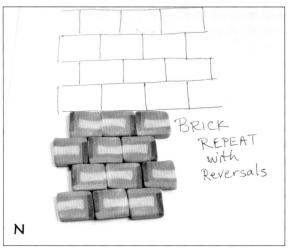

BRICK REPEAT with Reversals

N

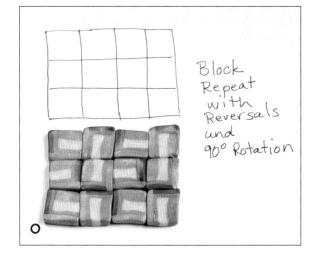

Block Repeat with Reversals and 90° Rotation

O

TIP ✳

A solid, baked base inside a sheet that has been rolled to a uniform thickness allows you to create very smooth forms, and shortens the sanding and finishing time later.

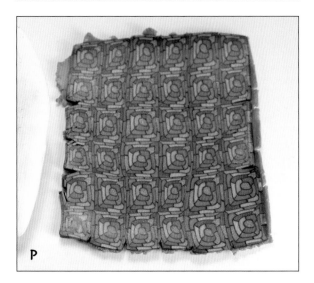

P

Q

R

S

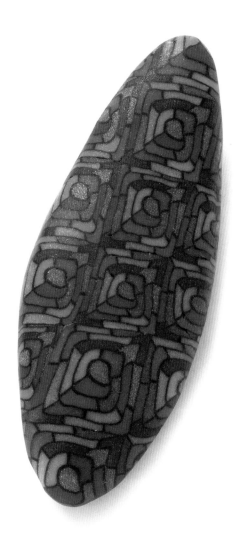

Cover irregular shapes with sheets of clay to form larger beads. I like to bake scrap clay into various shapes to be covered by sheets of caned pattern (P).

Cut two shapes of the pattern sheet to wrap around the base bead and just meet at the mid-line of the sides (Q, R). With the thin acrylic rod, carefully bring the two sides together and blend the seams (S).

SIMPLE CANES

STRIPED CANES Two-Color Stripe • Pinstripe • Multicolor Stripe • Blended Color Stripe • Combination Stripe • Ikat Stripe • Basket Weave • Log Cabin • Herringbone

CHECKERBOARD CANES Basic Checkerboard • Blended Checkerboard • Plaid

BULL'S-EYE CANES Simple Bull's-Eye • Square Bull's-Eye • Colorful Bull's-Eye • Complex Bull's-Eye

SPIRAL CANES Simple Spiral • Radial Spiral • Blended Spiral • Greek Key Spiral Variation

These very useful basic canes form the foundation for a wide variety of polymer clay bead and jewelry patterns. They include the striped, the checkerboard, the bull's-eye, and the spiral. I'll explore the basic formulas for these canes first, then I'll propose a few variations.

I enjoy cooking and I read a lot of recipes. However, I rarely follow a recipe when I get into the kitchen. I'm confident that if I understand the principles and the basic ingredients in a dish, the seasoning or additions are up to me. Think of these projects like that. I'll show you what I did, but there are no rules or no right cane pattern when it's your turn.

Because I want you to learn the process and not be concerned with perfectly replicating each cane, I don't always give exact clay amounts or color formulas. Sometimes I make small canes that are only enough for one project. You might really like a design and want to make a bigger cane so you will have more of it to use in a string of beads. Please adapt the recipe as you go. You'll have variations in results, and those variations, with practice, will help you in the development of your personal style. So if your cane doesn't look exactly like the one pictured, it's OK. Yours will be lovely, too!

Also, remember that this is not a project book. I want to show you techniques and inspire you with many variations. I complete some projects, but some of the designs I demonstrate will remain as unfinished beads or pendant parts. I want to give you lots and lots of ideas for the many ways canes can be used. Feel free to move a cane further in the reduction/ recombination process than I do, try your own color combinations, or try a different bead than I might have. As you explore caning in this book, you will build a collection of pattern canes. Eventually, we will combine some of the many patterns into more complex and sophisticated jewelry designs. So let's get started!

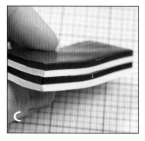

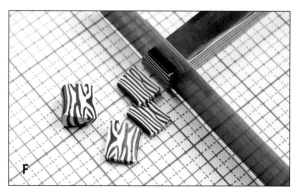

Striped Canes

The simplest cane, in my opinion, is a striped block made from equal-sized stacked sheets. When clay layers are hand-formed, the cane has a more irregular, organic feel. When layers are precisely rolled by pasta machine, the patterns are sharp and geometric.

Because of my background in textiles and clothing, I often treat my canework as fabric, slicing up canes and laying them in repeat to make sheets of pattern.

The variations I introduce later in this section mimic common and traditional fabric types, such as basket weave, herringbone, and ikat.

Two-Color Stripe

Let's begin with a two-color stripe of high contrast and equal thickness layers:

1 On the thickest pasta machine setting, roll two colors of clay to sheets of equal size (**A**).

2 Stack one layer on top of the other, lining up the edges and making sure not to trap air between the layers. Cut the stacked layers into two equal pieces (**B**).

3 Stack the two pieces to create a simple cane of four stripes (**C**).

4 Reduce the cane and cut it into equal pieces (**D**).

5 Repeat step 4 to make a cane with 16 stripes (**E**).

6 Remember that after reducing a cane, there will likely be some distortion, especially on the ends. Trim off as much of the end as necessary, a little at a time, until you've exposed the undistorted pattern (**F**).

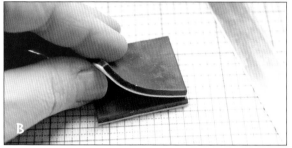

Pinstripe

OK, so an equal black and white stripe alone isn't very interesting. Set this cane aside for later. Let's try a variation on the same basic cane:

1 Roll one color into a sheet on the thickest pasta machine setting. Roll the second color several settings thinner. Place the thick sheet on the thin one and trim the pieces to equal size (**A**).

2 Cut and stack the layers (**B**).

3 Repeat the cutting and stacking until the cane has as many stripes as you want (**C**).

I made a pair of pinstripe earrings with this cane. Let me show you how to make the bead:

4 Roll a bit of scrap clay into a log. Cut two or three thin slices from the cane and wrap them around the cane with the stripe running the length of the bead (**D**).

5 Blend the seams and pinch the ends, keeping the stripes as straight as possible and bringing them to a point (**E**).

6 For earrings, add some decorative bead endcaps and pierce the length of the bead. Bake the beads with the endcaps in place. Finish as desired with headpins, accent beads, and earring wires. (The endcaps won't stick to the clay during baking, but placing them helps the bead hold its shape.)

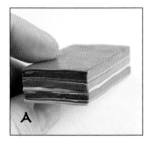
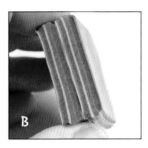

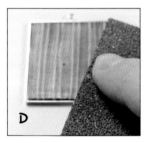
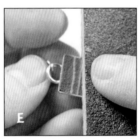

Multicolored Stripe

A black-and-white color palette is sophisticated and always in style, but you'll want to explore further variations in stripes and add color. I love that there are so many more options in jewelry findings these days—including bezel shapes that can be filled with polymer clay. A bracelet and pendant kit with square bezels is perfect for the following cane.

1 Mix five or six coordinating colors of clay for a cane. My palette consists of colors that are reduced a bit in saturation and have some metallic or pearl color added as well. Roll the clay colors into sheets and vary them between the thickest setting and a medium setting on the pasta machine (**A**).

2 Reduce and restack the cane once (**B**).

3 Cut slices of the cane as thick as needed to fill the bezel depth (**C**).

4 Instead of sanding and polishing, try texturing these stripes. Fill the bezel shape and then press firmly over the surface with a clean sanding sponge with a medium grit (**D**). Pressing with the sponge also allows you to make sure the clay fills the space all the way to the edges (**E**).

Bake the clay in the bezels, but after it is cured and has cooled, remove the striped squares, add a drop of glue to the bezel, and replace the square. I thought it was fun to alternate the stripe directions in the bracelet links to add just a little more interest to the design.

TIP ✳

This little composition shows that colors will always go together when they are derived from the same original colors. The colors on each end of the strip are the scraps from the stripe cane. The scraps were blended together until a new, uniform color was created. Instant color coordination! If only my wardrobe were so easy!

30

Blended Color Stripe

Remember learning the Skinner blend (p. 18)? When the shaded color of a blended sheet is used in a stripe cane, the effects are softened. Instead of a clean and graphic line, the look is a little more natural and muted.

1 Develop a blended sheet with three colors using the widest setting on the pasta machine. It doesn't have to be a really big blend; a sheet about 3x4 in. will do (**A**).

2 Rotate the blend 90 degrees and roll it through a medium setting on the pasta machine to lengthen the blend (**B**).

3 Trim the ends straight and cut the sheet into equal-width strips, about ½–¾-in. wide (**C**).

4 Stack the strips from left to right, keeping each strip in order (**D**).

5 Here is the basic cane, which can be used in many combinations (**E**).

6 I cut the cane into thirds, and stacked with the center piece rotated so that the same colors would meet (**F**).

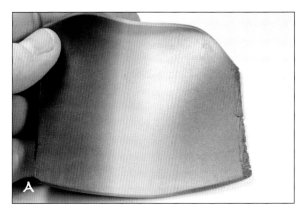

A

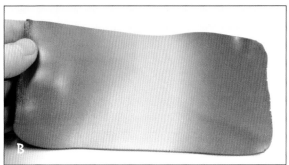

B

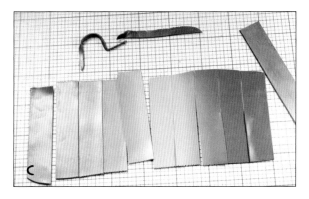

C

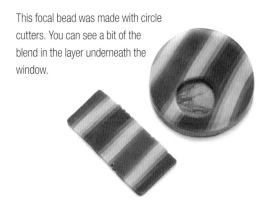

This focal bead was made with circle cutters. You can see a bit of the blend in the layer underneath the window.

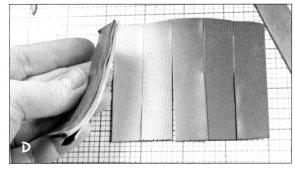

D

TIP ✳

When a cane is smaller than the intended shape, cut a thicker slice and roll it thinner.

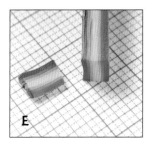

E

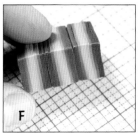

F

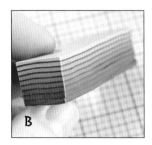

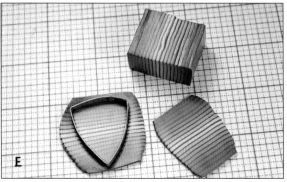

Combination Stripe

Next, let's try a variation that combines the concepts from the pinstripe and the blended color canes.

1 Start with a Skinner blend of two colors. This looks particularly good with a light neutral color on one end and a more saturated color for the other. Pair this with a dark color for the stripe (it does not have to be black—try blending a muddy neutral by adding the complementary color to the main color). I made a dark, muddy purple for my stripe color. Roll the stripe color very thin and roll the Skinner blend on the thickest setting. Layer the blend over the dark, being sure not to trap air (**A**).

2 Trim around the layers. Repeat steps 2–4 from Blended Color Stripe (p. 31). The stack should shade from light to dark with a dark stripe between each layer (**B**).

3 My dark stripe ended up on the bottom, so in order to preserve the stripe pattern, I rolled a very thin sheet of the stripe to add to the light side of one half (**C**).

4 Here's the cane put together so it shades from dark to light to dark (**D**).

5 You can make a pair of earrings with slices of this cane. Take a thicker slice and roll it a little to make it wide enough for your shape (**E**).

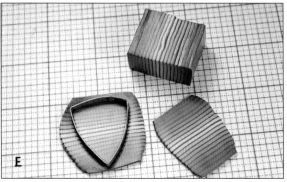

32

Ikat Stripe

Ikat (pronounced ee-kat) is a textile term that refers to a traditional fabric dyeing technique for woven fabric. In ikat patterns, the warp and weft (vertical and horizontal) threads are tied and dyed before they are threaded into the loom and woven. Because the color is applied to the threads before weaving, ikat patterns are characterized by a feathery or irregular lines between one color and another. Ikat can be mimicked in polymer by arresting the progress of a Skinner blend after only a couple passes through the pasta machine.

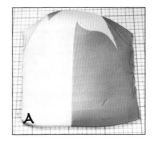
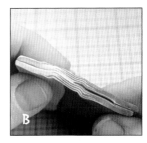
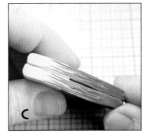
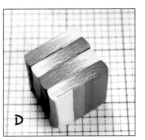

1 One very traditional style of ikat uses indigo (dark denim) dyes on unbleached cotton. To imitate this, start with a cream color and dark denim blue. I used an equal mix of pearl, ecru, and white for the cream color and added some silver to the blue to get a little metallic shimmer. Set up and begin a Skinner blend sheet about 3x4 in. using the thickest setting on the pasta machine. Stop blending after three or four repetitions of folding and rolling through the pasta machine. The colors should not have begun to blend much at all (**A**).

2 Cut the clay in half across the width of the sheet and stack the pieces. The clay will be much wider than the intended cane, so press the sheet edges inward toward the center while you stretch the cane lengthwise (**B**).

3 Continue to press the cane inward. Cut it in two and repeat the process when the cane is long enough to comfortably handle. Stack the pattern one more time, keeping the same colors adjacent to each other (**C**).

4 Eventually, the cane will be long and narrow instead of wide and short. When you have reduced it to about 6 or 8 in., cut it into four equal pieces and stack them, alternating the colors as shown (**D**).

5 Here are six slices of the cane arranged so the colors line up and the pattern continues across the seams (**E**).

6 Since the pattern is so vertical, I thought I would contrast it with a triangle shape and shift the direction of the pattern to the diagonal. This might become a focal bead or a pendant (**F**).

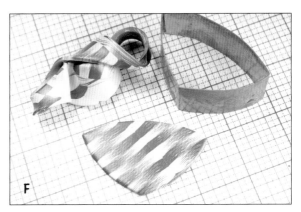

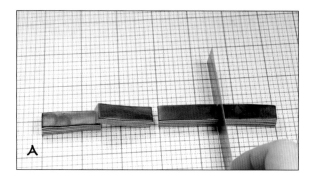

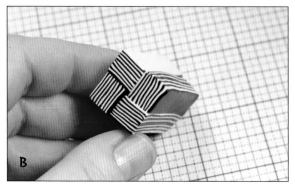

Combining cane patterns in the same colors is easy. This pendant combines the basket weave and a bit of the pinstripe cane from earlier. It's finished with a metal embellishment.

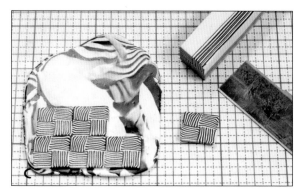

The next three variations of the stripe cane are a little more complex in the arrangement of the stripe unit in the reduction and repetition process. The basic cane unit is either rotated or cut up to form a new orientation before it is repeated.

Basket Weave

First, let's grab that black and white stripe cane we made and set aside at the beginning of this chapter and use it to try the basket weave.

1 Reduce the stripe cane until it is about 6–8 in. long. Trim the ends, if necessary, and cut the cane into four equal parts (**A**).

2 Reassemble the four pieces into a new cane with the two opposite corner pieces rotated 90 degrees to the others (**B**).

3 When slices of this cane are laid on a backing sheet, the overall pattern is the simple basket weave if the patternof each slice is lined up in the same direction (**C**). You can reverse the patterns to achieve other variations, such as a 2:1 or 2:2 basket weave.

One of the design concepts that requires some attention and decision-making is scale. Scale in caning refers to the size of a pattern unit relative to the overall size and form of the entire design (such as a bead or pendant). Reducing a cane changes the scale of a pattern. Also remember that if a sheet of pattern is rolled thinner on the pasta machine, the scale of the pattern may change. Here is the basket weave pattern reduced to two different sizes. Combining design units in different scale can be the source of interesting design, even if the pattern unit is the same.

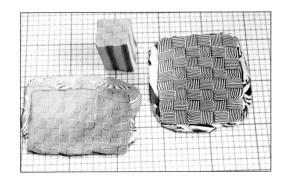

Log Cabin

Polymer often is used for faux treatments—faux stone, faux metal, and so forth. The following stripe cane is my faux version of a quilt pattern called the log cabin. Of course, the pattern can be imitated accurately in clay, but this manipulation of the stripe makes an interesting and very quick option.

1 Begin with a small piece of a multicolored stripe cane with a fairly high contrast and varied thicknesses. Turn the cane on its end and cut down the diagonal axis (**A**).

2 Rotate one half the cane end to end and reassemble into a square (**B**).

3 Reduce the cane, cut into four equal pieces and assemble with each unit in the same orientation (**C**).

4 Cut slices of the cane and arrange them on a backing sheet. The log cabin pattern is known for the illusion of depth that can be created by contrasting light against dark in the stripes. I think this cane achieves the same effect (**D**).

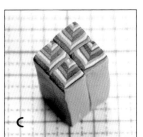

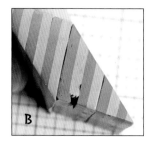

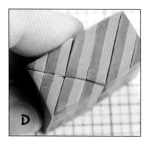

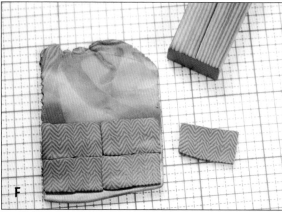

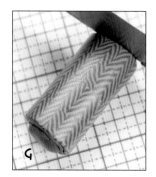

Herringbone

Our last stripe variation is another fabric pattern called herringbone. Herringbone is a twill weave variation with the diagonal line stripe reversed at a regular interval. Herringbone, usually a very subtle pattern, is common in men's suiting fabrics.

1 Begin with a two-color cane of equal width stripes. Turn the cane on its end and cut down the diagonal axis (**A**).

2 Rearrange the two pieces with the wide sides touching so that the stripe is continuous (**B**).

3 Cut off one end of the cane where a right angle intersects the side of the cane (**C**).

4 Move that triangular piece to the opposite end and line up the stripe with the main body of the cane. At this point, the cane should be a rectangular shape in two dimensions (**D**).

5 Reduce the cane and cut it into two pieces. Arrange the two pieces to form a chevron (**E**).

6 Reduce and recombine the cane as many times as desired and to the scale desired. Because I used very close values of colors, I cannot reduce the pattern much more than this before it would lose readability. This way, the pattern will be subtle (**F**).

7 Use the herringbone clay sheet to cover a tubular bead (**G**).

Checkerboard Canes

I never really followed the old "don't mix stripes and prints" rule in clothing selection. Such rules are made to be broken. In fact, mixing patterns is ultimately our goal. We began with stripes; next we'll make the checkerboard. And again, I find it fun to take pattern inspiration from fabric, so we will explore checks and plaid as well.

Basic Checkerboard

We just mastered the stripe cane. The next technique to learn is the checkerboard cane. Unless your checkerboard will be only a four- or nine-block pattern, it will be easiest to begin with a stripe cane.

1 Begin with equal sheets of black and white clay rolled at the thickest pasta machine setting. Create a striped stack of eight layers.

2 Turn the stack onto one side so the cross-section of stripe is facing front. Cut eight slices, slightly thicker than the width of the stripe, from the cane across the stripes (**A**). Roll each slice through the pasta machine on the thickest setting with the stripe aligned vertically into the rollers. This will ensure that all rows are equal in thickness and the squares will, in fact, be square. Arrange the rolled slices together reversing the light and dark positions in each row (**B**).

3 Repeat until all eight slices are arranged into an 8x8 (64-square) checkerboard (**C**). Compress the cane enough to consolidate it and eliminate any air spaces.

4 Use cane slices (**D**) to make a bead. Roll a log of scrap clay about ⅜ in. in diameter and roll two cane slices around it (**E**).

5 Time to break those rules and mix the checkerboard and stripe! I added a band of a pinstripe cane along one end (**F**).

6 After rolling to blend the seams, roll the log smooth and trim the ends (**G**). Pierce and bake.

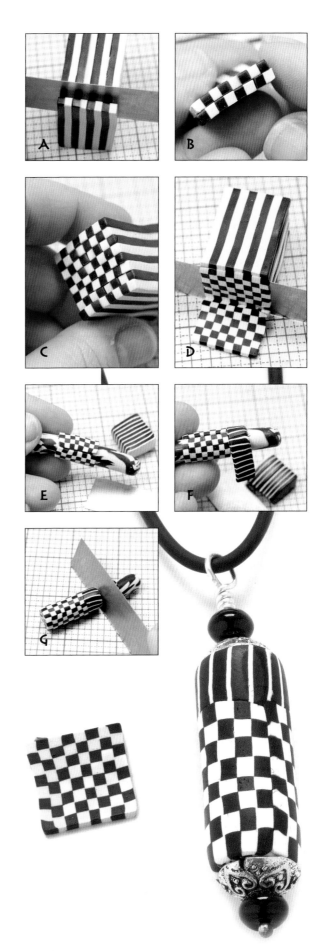

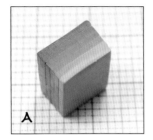

A

B

C

Blended Checkerboard

Let's try the same process with a blended cane.

1 Create a Skinner blend of two colors rolled on the thickest pasta machine setting for a sheet about 3x4 in. Cut the sheet into six equal strips, and stack for a blended stripe cane (**A**).

2 Cut six slices slightly thicker than the pasta machine's thickest setting (**B**).

3 Roll each slice through the pasta machine with the stripe held vertically. Stack the slices, reversing the color pattern in each layer (**C**).

4 Here's a look at the clean cut across the cane (**D**).

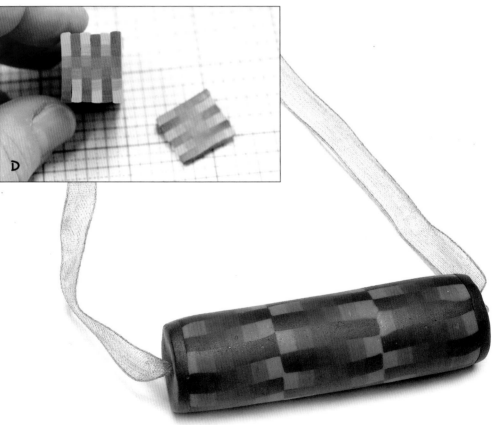

D

5 Take a look at two possible pattern layouts: On the top, the cane slices are reversed so that the same solid colors meet. On the bottom, the canes are arranged in a straight block repeat with the solid colors alternating **(E)**. See the difference? Which do you prefer?

6 I chose the second pattern. I created a full sheet of the pattern and rolled the seams closed **(F)**.

7 Roll a big fat log of scrap clay and wrap the pattern around it. So the scrap doesn't show, finish it with punched circles of solid color on the ends of the bead **(G)**.

8 Here's a view of the pierced bead ready to go into the oven **(H)**. Because of the blended color, it reminds me a bit of a woven check where the alternating colors of warp and weft create different shades of monochromatic check.

TIP ✳

When slicing canes, make sure your blade is sharp. Old, dull blades will cause smearing and more distortion of the shape as you slice. Wiping the blade with a wet-wipe helps make a blade cut clean and easily.

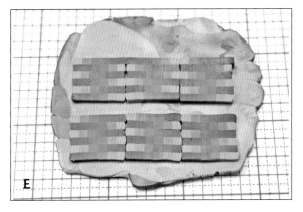

E

F

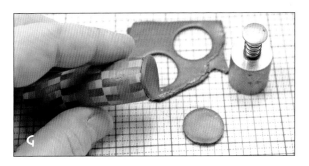

G

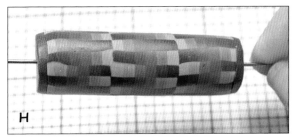

H

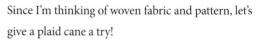

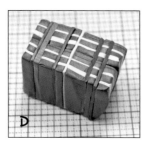

Plaid

Since I'm thinking of woven fabric and pattern, let's give a plaid cane a try!

1 Begin with a stripe cane of 3–5 colors and alternate the thickness of the layers. My starting stripe cane is approximately ¾x1x2 in. (**A**).

2 Reduce the cane by about half, trim the ends, cut it into two equal pieces, and reassemble (**B**).

3 Cut the cane into several pieces, cutting across the stripes and varying the width of the slices (**C**).

4 Roll additional sheets of various thicknesses of the colors used. Add the sheets between each of the cut slices. You can stack a couple of colors together occasionally to add variety (**D**).

5 Reduce the cane, cut into four, and reassemble (**E**).

TIP ✳

Because of my penchant for making repeat patterns of my canes, I rarely border my canes. However, it is a good technique and especially useful when a cane design represents a scene or when a single slice becomes a finished product (bead or pin or whatever). One of my favorite times to border canes is when I make mini-quilt pattern canes.

Here's a simple cane that was developed from some leftover cane pieces (**1**). I wrapped a very thin layer of one color around the cane and trimmed the ends to just meet (**2**). I then added a second, slightly thicker sheet of color around the first (**3**). The two layers of border can act in the same way as a matte and frame around a design. These two finished slices (**4**) will make a nice, simple pair of earrings.

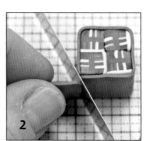

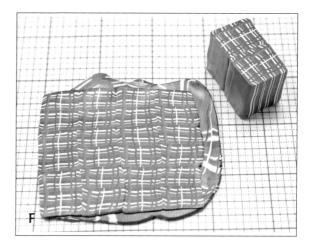

6 Since we're imitating a fabric, let's lay out a big sheet of cane slices over scrap clay (**F**). Love that!

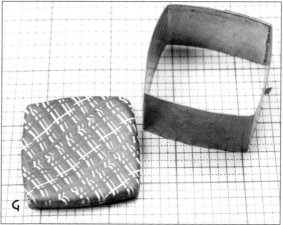

7 Cut the shape (**G**). To make a pendant, add the scrap layer on the back to give the piece some heft.

8 After baking the pattern piece, add some solid background over the back and sides to frame it. Insert and glue a bail finding into this layer (**H**).

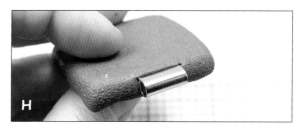

9 Texture the backing/framing layer (**I**) for an interesting surface contrast. It doesn't need to be sanded later.

10 Finally, trim the front edge smooth with the front surface. After baking, sand the surface smooth and polish it for a wonderful finish.

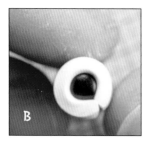

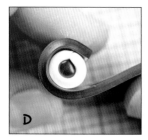

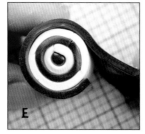

Bull's-Eye Canes

The bull's-eye cane is more versatile than you may think. The simple concentric circles are always an effective design element. I use variations of the bull's-eye cane often as the basis for a more complex pattern. It can be reshaped and repeated into some unusual and interesting designs. Let's explore the simple bull's-eye in black and white, and I'll share a few construction tips along the way.

Simple Bull's-Eye

1 Begin with a smooth log of black between ⅛–¼ in. in diameter. Using the thickest setting on the pasta machine, roll a sheet of white about 1½–2-in. wide. Place the black log on the white sheet and trim its length equal to the width of the sheet (**A**).

2 Wrap the white around the black log. Make sure that both the inside and outside corners of the seam edges meet (**B**).

3 Smooth the seam with an acrylic rod (**C**).

4 With the pasta machine, roll a black sheet the same width. Wrap it around the white layer (**D**).

TIP ✳

To determine where to cut, roll the clay around the log slightly past a full revolution. The leading corner of the cut edge will make a mark on the sheet when it touches. Unroll the log slightly. There should be a faint line across the clay. Cut inside the mark by an amount equal to the thickness of the sheet.

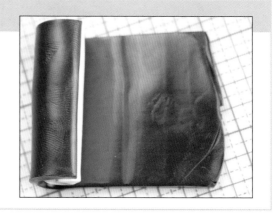

5 Continue adding contrasting layers for as many concentric circles as desired (**E**).

6 When reducing the log, spend more time pinching and squeezing from the center toward the ends (**F**) than rolling the clay against the work surface. Rolling against the work surface will warm the outer clay more than the inside. The warmer, softer clay will move more quickly than the interior and contribute to more distortion of the cane and more scrap or waste on the ends.

7 Here are three slices of the cane reduced at different scales. I cut the smallest piece into fat slices for pierced beads (**G**).

8 Since the pattern is so simple, I used repetition of the element in these earrings. The long shape also contrasts with the pattern (**H**).

9 Simple works in color also. This cane used four colors with layers of varied thicknesses. Just pierce thick slices to make beads (**I**).

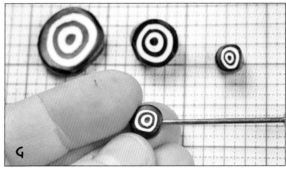

Square Bull's-Eye

Keeping things simple can result in an effective design, but let's move on and come up with some variations with these canes. A good principle to learn and always remember is this: Canes can morph from shape to shape. We can start with a cane in a round log and convert it to a triangle or square loaf. That's when it gets fun!

1 Take a piece of the black-and-white bull's-eye cane and convert it to a square: Pinch and roll the cane into a square while reducing it. Cut it into four for a block repeat (**A**).

2 This pendant will play back and forth between circles and squares. Create a sheet of pattern from the four-block cane. Cut a circle from the pattern sheet and punch out a square from that. Texture a sheet of black with the sanding block and lay the circle over it. Re-cut the circle through all the layers (**B**).

3 After baking and sanding, drill through the pendant with a ⅛-in. bit hand drill for a cord hole.

44

A

B

Colorful Bull's-Eye

Now let's add color. Begin with a very simple bull's-eye that uses each color only once. All of these colors have lots of metallic in the mix. Square up a piece of the cane and set it into a block repeat (**A**). Let's use this pattern for another pendant bead.

I think this cane would look good with a metal accent or layers (**B**). Look for another design using this cane on p. 92 of the gallery. (Can you tell it was a fairly large cane to begin?)

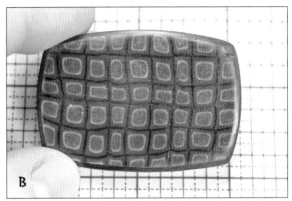

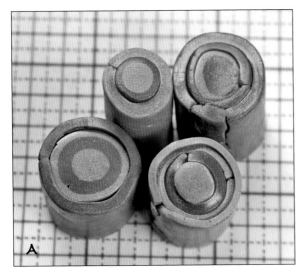

A

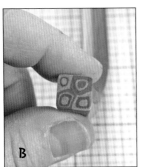

B

C

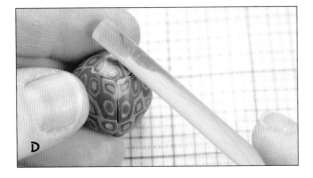

D

Complex Bull's-Eye

1 Up to this point, we've repeated the same element. Next, let's make several bull's-eye canes with the same color scheme, but vary the arrangement of colors and the thickness of layers (**A**).

2 Compress the cluster of canes into a square cane. Reduce the cane (**B**).

3 Cut the reduced cane into four and reassemble it into another block (**C**). I played a bit with the arrangement and rotation of the canes to make a less regular pattern.

4 Make a 1-in. diameter ball from scrap clay. Cut slices from the cane to cover, and blend the seams (**D**).

5 I liked that bead, but decided to try compressing it into a lentil shape (**E**).

6 Yes, this will be pretty as a focal bead pendant, so let's pierce it through for baking (**F**).

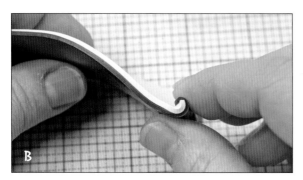

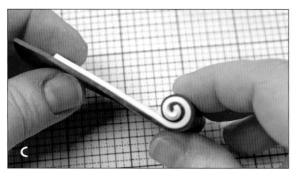

Spiral Canes

Here's a clay riddle: What do you get when you cross a stripe cane with a bull's-eye cane? A spiral! Well, OK, maybe I shouldn't attempt comedy… While my attempt at humor might be considered a little lame (my kids would say very lame!), there's a little truth in my story. A spiral cane made with a blended sheet will come closer to a bull's-eye cane because it is a progression of concentric circles of color but without hard edges separating them. A spiral using multiple contrast color sheets rolled up into a log will have more similarities to an alternating stripe.

Simple Spiral
Let's begin again with black and white:

1 Roll a sheet of black and a sheet of white on medium thickness to about 2x3 in. Lay one color on top of the other; trim away ⅛ in. on one end and ½ in. on the other (**A**).

2 On the end where the top layer is ⅛ in. shorter, begin curling the bottom layer over the top, rounding the edge and rolling evenly across the width (**B**).

3 Firmly continue rolling the length of the sheets (**C**). Be careful not to leave air pockets between the layers.

4 Finish the spiral and blend the cut edge into the surface (**D**).

5 To reduce this cane, remember to pinch, compress, and stretch from the center outward more than you roll. Roll only as necessary to keep the shape uniform.

Try creating a composition to put in a bezel-pendant finding. Because the effect of the black and white is very graphic, I think a novelty print placement will be fun.

6 Roll very thin slices of the cane into a background of solid black (**E**).

7 Add another element that continues the theme: How about a row of checks? Take a thin slice from a stripe cane and then cut thin strips across the stripe. Using little pieces of check end-to-end is a good technique for borders, edges, separating patterns, etc. (**F**).

8 Cut the shape needed to fill the bezel and apply the shape. Rolling across the clay ensures that the piece will expand to fill the bezel area (**G**).

9 Bake the piece in the bezel. After the clay cools, carefully pry it out of the bezel. Sand the piece. Place a drop of superglue in the bezel and replace the piece in the bezel.

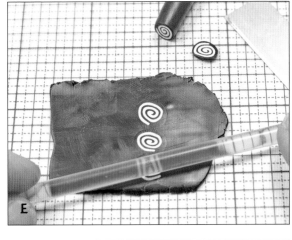

E

F

G

A

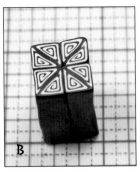

B

C

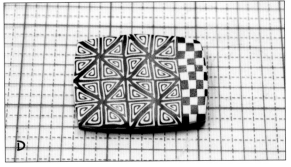

D

Radial Spiral

Now, let's try morphing another piece of our original spiral to take a cane in another direction.

1 Press the cylinder into a triangle and cut the cane in two. Place them together into a square (**A**).

2 Reduce, cut, and reassemble another square. Set the pattern into a radial arrangement (**B**). Another option is to position all dominant diagonals in the same direction.

3 I like the pattern. It's simple, so how about combining it with another black and white pattern (**C**)?

4 Here's the piece cut into a shape appropriate for a pin or a focal pendant. Back the pattern with a thick sheet of scrap clay to add some depth. Finish it with a textured black back and border (**D**).

TIP ✳

When using a purchased metal bail, plan to embed the bail at some intermediate stage of the construction of the piece. This bail was glued onto the back of the design pattern layer after it was baked. The bail is applied with superglue. Then, the outside textured black layer was added. Combining glue and embedding the piece between layers of clay helps add to the strength of the connection.

A

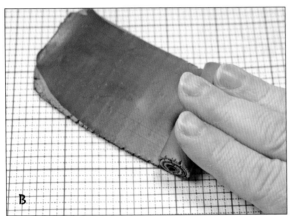

B

C

Blended Spiral

Now it's time to work in color! My favorite plan is always to start with a Skinner blend.

Next, let's combine the two concepts together: a spiral with a Skinner blend and a solid layer.

1 Begin with a thick sheet of blended color and layer a thin sheet of solid color on top (**A**).

2 Rotate the sheet 90 degrees from its original blend orientation into the pasta machine and thin it to a medium setting. Roll the sheet in a spiral (**B**).

3 This spiral is very tight with many layers because of the length and thickness of the sheets (**C**). Vary these aspects for different effects.

TIP ✳

When rolling a Skinner blend into a spiral, the thickness of the sheet and the width of the blend will influence the effect. When a blended sheet is short, there will be a greater degree of color change as it is rolled into a spiral and each layer contacts subsequent concentric layers. If the blend is dramatic and short, each layer will be distinct. If you want a very subtly blended spiral, it is helpful to rotate the blended sheet 90 degrees and roll the sheet on a couple of progressively thinner settings. In this case, the gradation of color is more gradual from the center outward.

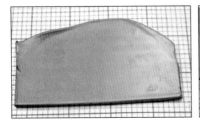

4 Reduce a piece of this cane to just under ½ in. in diameter. Layer slices of this spiral in a random, organic fashion on a sheet of solid color (**D**).

5 After creating the sheet and rolling it smooth, cut two circles and cover a baked lentil shape bead (**E**).

6 Smoothing the seams together with a rod hides the seam and gives a professional finish (**F**). Pay attention to the smoothness before baking so you won't spend as much time sanding later.

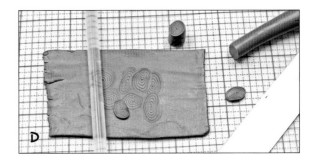

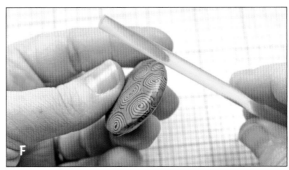

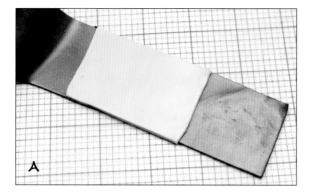

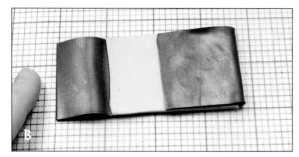

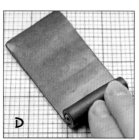

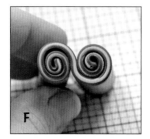

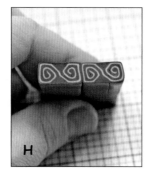

Greek Key Spiral Variation

Let's explore one more variation. Rolling a spiral halfway from each end creates a swirl element that resembles a Greek key pattern.

1 Start with high-contrast colors rolled to a medium thickness on the pasta machine. Roll one sheet twice as long as the other, but make the sheets equal in width (**A**).

2 Arrange the sheets so the shorter sheet can be folded within the longer sheet. First fold one side over the contrast color (**B**).

3 Fold the second side over the contrast color and trim the ends to just meet (**C**).

4 This strip of clay will now be three layers. Rotate the piece so the length is positioned at 90 degrees to the pasta machine and roll it though on the widest setting. Note the length of the strip, and make a small mark at the halfway point. Begin to roll up the spiral (**D**).

5 Flip the roll over and begin to roll the other end into a spiral (**E**).

6 Continue rolling both ends of the spiral until they meet at the halfway mark (**F**).

7 Form a log of the outside color and press it into a triangle shape. Cut two lengths of the triangle log the length of the cane and apply them to fill the space of the S-shape (**G**).

8 Square up the sides and ends of the cane and reduce and repeat it once (**H**). This is a great pattern to use in a composition of multiple patterns as a border or divider.

COMPLEX CANES

COMBINATION CANES	Black and White • Colored Combinations
KALEIDOSCOPE CANES	Six Point Pattern • Radial Square • Brain
FLORAL CANES	Simple Flower • Leaf and Stem • Arrangement • Morning Glory • Rose • Bouquet
TRANSLUCENT CANES AND OVERLAY PATTERNS	Floating Geometrics • Line Drawing • Translucent Color Blend

We began our exploration with simple individual canes and experimented with variations of the individual elements of color, scale, and the repetitive patterns created in reducing and reassembling canes. Now we will make individual canes that can be combined for more complex patterns and color schemes. If you have lots of pieces left from the previous exercises, then you are ready to go. That's the fun part about caning. Canes can continually be morphed, combined, and reduced until they are used in beautiful beads.

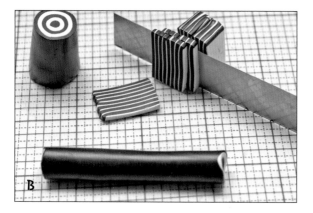

Combination Canes

Combination canes are built from basic cane units. Begin by looking over your collection of black-and-white canes to see what you can combine. If you don't have a few inches of each of several canes, take a few moments and make up some stripe, spiral, check, or bull's-eye canes. Since you know the basics now, my instructions will be somewhat more demonstrative of possibilities rather than instructive. Remember my analogy about cane-making being like cooking without following a recipe too closely? I'll show you what I've done, but you should definitely consider this a very flexible recipe: You can choose what elements and how much of each to use as you like.

Black-and-White Combination

1 Here are pieces of each of the basic cane styles (**A**).

2 Reduce a section of the bull's-eye cane until it is about ½ in. in diameter and 2–3 in. long. Then, cut slices of the stripe cane to combine with it (**B**).

3 Each piece must be the same length to fit together. To create interest, begin a repeat of an element (**C**).

4 The whole checkerboard is too big of a pattern, relative to the other elements—so cut the cane in half and use one piece. Add a compressed spiral element to fill in the corner (**D**).

5 The cane is ready to compress to consolidate it and reduce it as much as desired (**E**).

6 A ½x¾-in. slice is perfect for building a hair clip. Here's a row of slices laid out in the size needed for a 4-in. French clip (**F**).

7 Roll the seams, trim the edges straight, and apply the strip to the clip. After baking, sanding, and polishing, glue the clay to the metal finding.

8 What else can be made from this cane? Here's a sheet of the pattern laid in block repeat with a reversal (**G**).

9 Since the pattern is pretty active, a bit of a more simple contrast pattern will give the eye a place to rest. Add a strip of pinstripe beside the busy pattern and cut a shape for a pendant from the sheet (**H**). Back the shape with some scrap clay for a bit more thickness. After baking, add textured black on the back and edges.

Look for a pair of earrings with this pattern in the gallery on p. 87.

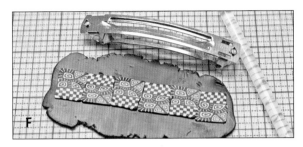

F

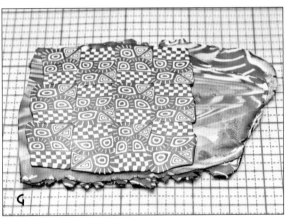

G

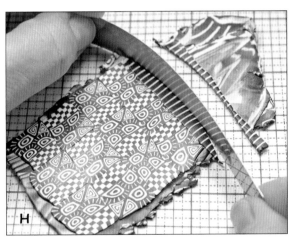

H

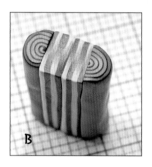

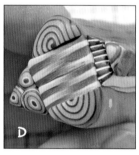

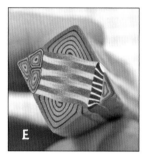

Colored Combination Version 1

Now, we'll go through the same process of building a cane from some of the colored cane variations.

1 Begin with a big chunk of the ikat cane, a couple of bull's-eye canes, and a spiral (**A**).

2 Reduce and double the piece of ikat and then split the spiral to fit around it (**B**). As you begin assembling, keep an eye on the scale of the patterns. If a pattern will look too big compared with the others, go ahead and just use part of the cane and reduce it to fit.

3 Next, reduce one of the bull's-eye canes, repeat it, and morph it into a triangle. The overall shape is coming together in a square (**C**).

4 Here, I'd planned to use the blue and olive bull's-eye cane. It wasn't big enough to fill the remaining space, so I added a little something more. I like to add some black and white into colored canes as well; it provides a good graphic effect (**D**).

5 Consolidate and trim the cane to see how it looks (**E**). Decide if you like the shape and think about what will happen when it's put into repeat.

6 Since the cane has a strong diagonal direction, decide if the cane will be repeated in straight block or rotated. Leaving it in simple block makes the single cane square the repeat element (**F**). Rotating the cane pieces turns the entire four-square block into the repeat unit.

TIP ✳

Sometimes I will morph a cane into a new shape, such as a triangle or rectangle, and mirror it at this point.

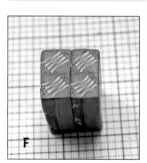

58

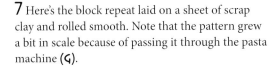

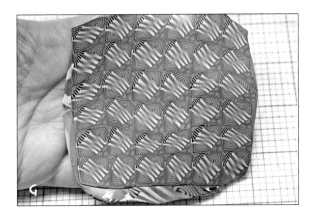

7 Here's the block repeat laid on a sheet of scrap clay and rolled smooth. Note that the pattern grew a bit in scale because of passing it through the pasta machine (**G**).

8 Cut circles from this sheet and apply them to a lightbulb to form lentil beads (**H**).

9 After baking the circles on the bulb, remove them and fill the concave space with scrap clay (**I**).

10 Cover the scrap clay with a layer of solid color that coordinates with the pattern side (**J**).

11 Texture the solid back (**K**).

12 Pierce the bead through the soft clay, keeping the hole as close to the edge of the lentil as possible (**L**).

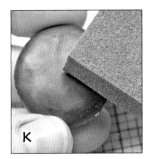

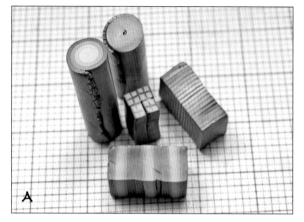

A

Complex Color Combination Version 2

Aren't these canes just a whole lot of lovely fun? Let's try one more, and I'm going to be even more intentionally adventurous about morphing the canes from shape to shape.

1 Collect another group of cane pieces to put together (**A**).

2 Start with a color blended stripe cane. Use two-thirds of it and press it into a triangle while you reduce it to a few inches long. This will be the central element in the composition (**B**).

3 Roll the windowpane of yellow and brown into a circle and add it to the triangle (**C**).

4 Repeating an element is a good idea to use regularly. It also helps with scale. Make the blue blended spiral into a row of dots (**D**).

5 Square them up and add them to the growing cane (**E**).

6 To better fit this evolving design, cut the next piece in half (**F**).

7 Both pieces fit well this way (**G**). Remember to reduce elements as you go along so they are the same length as the rest of the cane.

8 Finally, complete the cane shape by filling in with a little log of spiral cane (**H**).

9 I decided to compress the teardrop shape into a triangle and repeat it (**I**).

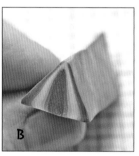

B

C

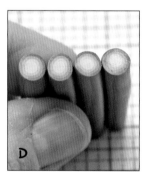

D

E

F

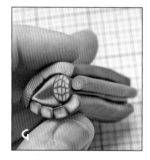

G

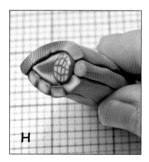

H

I

Here are some options for a repeat: Put different sides and angles together (**J**), or create a mirror version (**K**).

10 Press the mirror cane into a triangle and mirror it again (**L**).

11 Let's make beads from this cane pattern. It is easiest to make cane slices fit a circle if the core bead diameter is just slightly larger than the width of the cane (**M**).

12 Cut six slices off the cane and press four of them around the diameter of the bead core (**N**).

13 Press the last two slices on the top and bottom of the bead as if it were the sides of a cube (**O**).

14 Blend the seams and smooth the bead (**P**).

15 For a lentil shape, flatten the bead (**Q**). Pierce before baking.

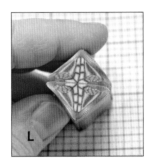
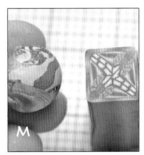
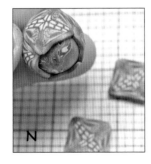

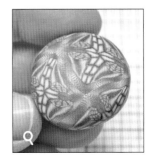

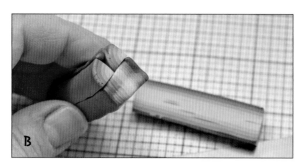

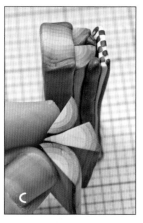

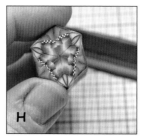

Kaleidoscope Canes

When I was a kid, I loved kaleidoscopes. All of mine were just plastic toys, but I loved to look through them, especially pointing them up toward sunlight to get brighter pattern images. As an adult, I realize that they can be very precisely made, and some become collector's items. And while I've never made one, I understand the concepts of mirrors and angles that make the magic happen.

Six-Point Pattern

True kaleidoscope patterns demonstrate a six-point pattern with mirror imaging along each axis. In order to develop a kaleidoscope pattern in polymer clay, we will work with equilateral triangles.

1 Begin with a grouping of basic canes that provides a fair amount of value contrast and has a harmonious color scheme (**A**).

2 Cut the rose-colored spiral into quarters, and combine with a piece of blended stripes. Fill in some of the space with some solid color (**B**).

3 Cut up another blended spiral and rearrange the pieces (**C**).

4 The composition is beginning to fill out (**D**).

5 Add a few more elements (**E**).

6 Finish the cane, consolidate it, and shape it into an equilateral triangle (**F**).

7 If the cane is large, cut it into two halves (**G**). Reserve one piece to manipulate in another pattern.

8 Reduce the cane, trim it, and cut it into six equal pieces. Explore different arrangements of mirroring by rotating or reversing the cane pieces. Here's one version (**H**).

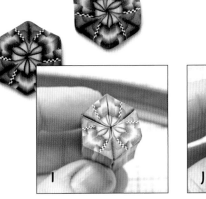

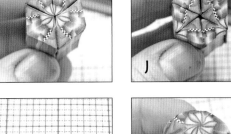

9 And another **(I)**.

10 And one more **(J)**.

11 Slices of a hexagon cane look lovely repeated. Does this remind you of soccer ball seams **(K)**?

12 Make a bead by wrapping the sheet around a baked form **(L)**.

Now, pick up the half cane you reserved earlier. The first kaleidoscope pattern is fairly simple and large. By reducing and repeating the cane once before setting it into a hexagon, you'll achieve a finer, more complex pattern.

1 Cut the cane into two pieces and repeat them **(M)**. (I chose not to mirror them here.)

2 Force the new shape into another triangle **(N)**.

3 Reduce the cane evenly, trim it, and cut it into six pieces. Here's one possible pattern **(O)**.

4 Here's another pattern option with a different set of axes mirrored **(P)**.

5 A hexagonal cane can be easily converted to a circle **(Q)**. This is a great pattern to put into a round bezel bracelet and pendant.

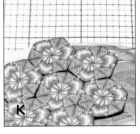

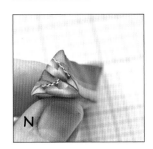

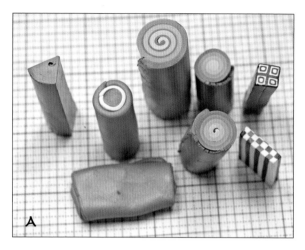

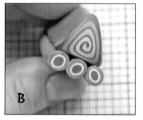

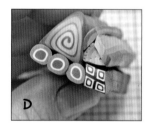

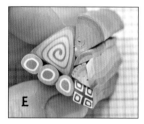

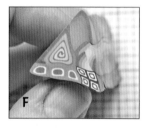

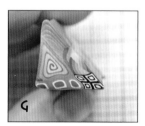

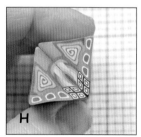

64

Radial Square Kaleidoscope

The kaleidoscope teaches the interesting principles of mirroring within a pattern. I love to apply the principles, but for some reason, I am more drawn to working with square canes. I find them more versatile for repeating. So let's repeat the process again, but instead of working with a hexagon, we'll create a radial square.

1 The initial cane palette (**A**).

2 To end up with a square, we need to begin with a triangle in order to create the diagonals (**B**).

3 This piece is going to fill a corner, so morph it into a diamond instead of a square (**C**).

4 Continue to mix color and value in the composition (**D**).

5 The composition is complete (**E**).

6 Compress and consolidate the cane (**F**).

7 It must also become a triangle (**G**).

8 Reduce the cane and cut it in half. Here's a mirror image arrangement (**H**).

9 In this option, one piece is rotated. Let's use this version (**I**).

10 Reduce the cane and set it into a four-block square. Mirror this pattern along both the horizontal and vertical axes (**J**).

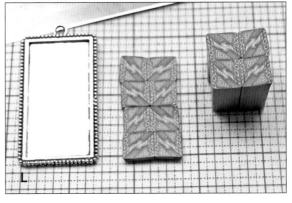

11 This option has a more dominant diagonal appearance. Each piece of cane is set 90 degrees to the ones adjacent to it (**K**).

12 It's time to use this cane in something. This metal bezel pendant will be pretty. Arrange the pattern to point toward a center point, as in Southwest Indian weaving patterns (**L**).

13 Bake the clay in the bezel. After baking, carefully pry the clay out, sand, trim clean on the edges, polish, and glue back in place with superglue (**M**).

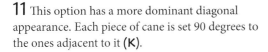

Here's another use of the cane. I've laid the slices from the 90-degree version on a backing sheet. I think it will need a contrasting element.

1 Remember the spiral cane that was at the center of the composition? A piece of it will be a good foil to the busy pattern (**N**).

2 That small spiral/square makes a nice second pattern. The elements and colors appear in both patterns, so there is a good repetition of design (**O**).

3 Here's the final composition. A solid blue stripe adds just a bit more separation to the patterns. Finish it with the same blue for a backing and border (**P**).

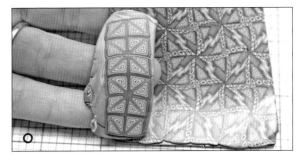

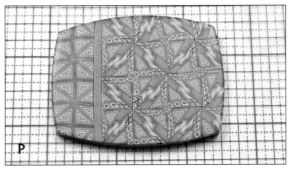

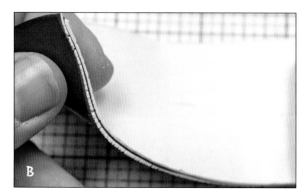

Brain

Another favorite cane of mine goes by many names. I've seen a number of variations of the same principle called "brain cane," "folded cane," or "squiggle cane." The basic idea is to have a sheet of stripe that is somewhat randomly folded up on itself in undulating or meandering lines. Some of these versions lay the stripe and the color blend together in one sheet. My version begins with a color blend rolled into a spiral with a separate sheet of stripe that will do the meandering.

Let me show you:

1 Begin with a rolled-up color blend of tan to brown and a stack of black and white. The black and white should be about 3 in. long and the same width as the length of the color blend (**A**).

2 Roll the black and white stack through the pasta machine, then repeat. Roll the four-layer stack to a medium setting so the stripes are fairly fine (**B**).

3 Cut the blend cane into several irregular shapes such as wedges and crescents. Make sure the cuts are parallel so the shapes are equal down their length (**C**).

4 Arrange a few pieces of the color blend around the black and white strip. Begin to fold the strip back and forth on itself and against the color pieces (**D**).

5 Continue folding the black and white and adding more color wedges (**E**).

6 Continue until all the color pieces are incorporated. If there is additional black-and-white strip, trim it off (**F**). Avoid wrapping the entire shape with the black and white, as this will create an unattractive boundary line around the cane.

7 Compress and reduce the cane. Aim to reduce it into a triangle. Trim, cut into two pieces, and arrange with a mirror orientation (**G**).

8 Reduce this cane again and cut into four pieces. Set the pieces into a square (**H**).

9 Apply six slices around a base ball of clay (**I**).

10 Flatten the finished bead (**J**). Bake it without piercing it. The hole can be drilled later with a hand drill, front to back through the center.

To finish the pendant as pictured above, pass the wire bail through the front, then up through a pewter bead frame and a brown glass bead. Finish at the top with a wrapped loop.

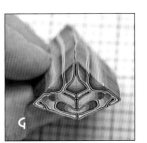

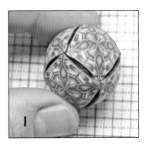

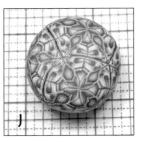

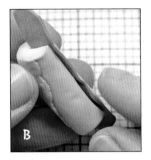
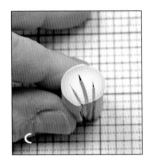
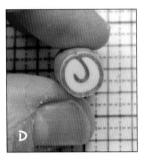
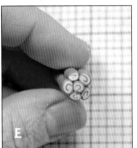

Floral Canes

Once you have mastered the basic canes, any subject becomes possible with the planning and combination of various elements. Canes containing pictures of objects can be reduced to shapes and parts, and assembled from the basic units that have been covered so far. Elaborate landscapes, portraits, animals, and lots of types of flowers are common themes for caners who like to put a lot of time and detail into realistic canes. Here, we'll briefly explore the subject of flowers.

Simple Flower

The most basic flower is a simple five- or six-petal flower. The petals are cylinders that are arranged around a center.

1 Begin with a blended spiral of white and cream. The cane should be about ½ in. in diameter and 4–5 in. long. Make an incision down the length of the cane at a depth about half the cane's diameter (**A**).

2 Mix a slightly darker shade for a contrast vein in the petals. I used a muddy taupe color. Roll a very thin piece and insert it into the incision in the cane (**B**).

3 Repeat with two more cuts into the length of the cane and insert more veins (**C**).

4 Next create a center for the flower. Begin with a short length of two shades of yellow or gold, and roll up a spiral. This can be a very small cane (**D**).

5 Reduce the spiral and cut it into six or seven equal pieces. Reassemble into a cluster (**E**).

6 Reduce the center cane to about ¼ in. in diameter. Reduce the petal cane until the petal diameter is slightly larger than the center. Be careful to keep the lines of the veins straight. Cut the petal into five equal pieces and arrange around the center with the veins touching the center (**F**).

Leaf and Stem

Next, let's make a leaf to go with the flowers. Begin with a shaded spiral of two colors of green. The spiral cane can be about ¾ in. in diameter and several inches long. Save a bit of the darker shade for veins. Reserve about a ½-in. piece of the spiral for making stems or branches later.

1 Make four or five parallel cuts down the length of the spiral cane (**A**). Roll some of the reserved dark color into a sheet on a very thin setting.

2 Cut pieces of the thin sheet to apply between each cut layer as the cane is reassembled. When all the layers are replaced and the cylinder is reassembled, make another vertical cut dividing the cane in half with the cut at about a 60-degree angle to the parallel lines (**B**).

3 Add a thin sheet of the dark color to one side. Rotate the other half of the cane and apply so that the lines now form a V shape (**C**).

4 Pinch the cane into a leaf shape (**D**).

5 Using the reserved piece of spiral cane, reduce it to about ¼ in. in diameter. Flatten the cylinder and roll it through the pasta machine parallel with the rollers to a medium thickness (**E**). This sheet will be used for the stem.

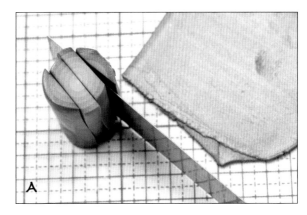

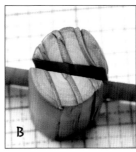

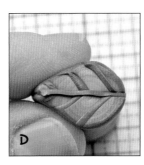

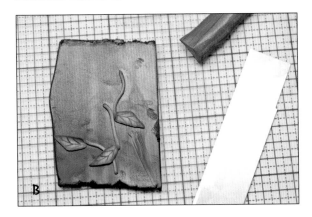

Arrangement

We now have a flower cane, a leaf cane, and a stem. It's time to make a floral arrangement, and then a brooch to show it off.

1 Choose a color or color blend sheet for a background and roll a sheet about 2x3 in. on the thickest setting. This background is a blend from silver to black. Begin by placing very thin slices from the stem sheet down the center of the background (**A**).

2 Add thinly sliced leaves (**B**).

3 Roll the leaves and stem into the background. A small diameter rod is especially useful for this (**C**).

4 Add thin slices of the flower cane and roll them into the background. Overlap elements occasionally for a more natural arrangement (**D**).

5 When the composition is satisfactory, cut a shape (**E**).

6 By making brooches concave, the pin construction is recessed. This helps a brooch lie flat against a garment instead of flopping over. Baking the clay over a convex surface like a lightbulb, or over a cylinder, such as an empty aluminum can, are good options. This is an expended floodlight bulb, so the curve is subtle (**F**).

7 I do not trust any glue to hold metal and polymer clay together without the assistance of a mechanical connection as well (embedded materials, enclosed spaces), so I press pinbacks into clay. Use a drop of liquid clay between the baked surface and the new clay. Then embed the pin finding (**G**).

8 Add another layer of clay over the pin bar and smooth the surfaces. I like to sign my work with a slice of my name cane, secured with a drop of liquid clay. Re-bake the pin. Sand and polish once cooled (**H**).

70

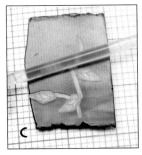

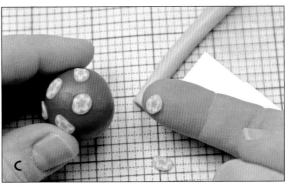

Sometimes irregular shapes like flower canes need to be reduced to be much smaller than their original size. When this is the case, it is useful to fill the irregular spaces with translucent clay in order to reduce a regular shape like a cylinder or rectangle. Let's do this with a section of the flower cane so it can be reduced much smaller.

1 Roll a snake of translucent clay about ¼ in. in diameter. Pinch it into a triangle and reduce it until it is the size of the open space between each petal. Cut five pieces the length of the flower cane and fill all the spaces (**A**).

2 Roll a thin sheet of translucent clay and wrap it completely around the flower cane, butting the edges and trimming clean (**B**).

3 Now the cane can be reduced to the desired size. Here, I've cut very thin tiny flowers and applied them to a contrast bead (**C**).

4 For another element on the bead, I added tiny dots of gold in clusters of three all around (**D**). Notice that the translucent border is slightly visible around the flowers. This will become a little less apparent after baking, but translucent is never completely transparent. This is why slicing as thin as possible is important. I pressed my bead into an oval lentil and pierced it for a focal bead.

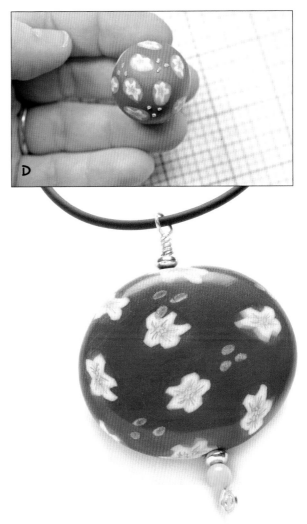

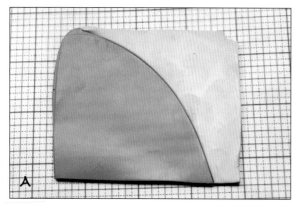

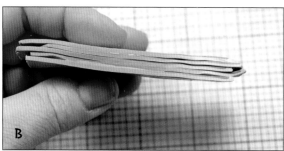

Morning Glory

One of my favorite flowers is the morning glory. Years ago, I had a vine that grew up the railing near an east-facing front porch step. I liked to sit on the steps in the morning with my coffee and admire my morning glories—the sunrise and the flowers. So let's give a morning glory a try in a cane.

1 Occasionally, a blended clay sheet will combine colors where one color has more influence or when the desired gradation should shift from a gradual to a rapid change. In these cases it is useful to use two fitted curves in the Skinner blend instead of equal right triangles of clay (**A**).

2 To create some of the veiny shading in the morning glory petals, stop the blend before it's completely blended. Cut the sheet into several layers and stack them with the sides aligned and the ends staggered, keeping the light color on one side and the blue on the other (**B**).

3 The stack will start out wide and short. Press inward from the sides as you pull and stretch the length to reduce the cane. Work it into a slight wedge shape (**C**). Trim the ends and cut into two pieces.

4 This morning glory has a strong star pattern with contrasting colors. Add a half-blended cane of purple/red/pink and enfold it in the reduced wedge of the petal (**D**).

5 Add a skinny snake of solid pink to the point of the wedge and continue to reduce the cane (**E**).

6 Cut the cane into five pieces and assemble them into a cylinder (**F**).

7 The petal indentations were lost when the cane was reduced. To correct this, press a needle tool down the length of the cane (**G**).

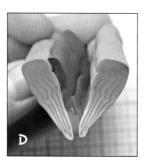

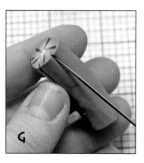

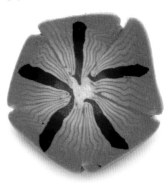

72

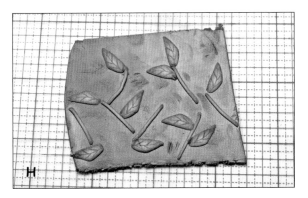

H

I

J

K

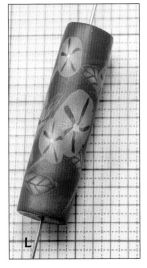

L

M

It's time to make something with the morning glories. This red and purple background presents an interesting design challenge: Use closely related colors from the cane pattern yet create enough contrast and harmony in the overall design.

8 Begin the composition with stems and leaves (**H**).

9 Add the flowers and roll them into the background. Notice that the flowers are reduced to different sizes and overlap each other to contribute a sense of perspective (**I**).

10 Let's create a big bead with this sheet. Roll a fat cylinder of scrap clay and pierce it. Don't remove the needle. Trim the leading edge of the sheet straight and begin rolling it around the scrap core (**J**).

11 Trim the ends to meet and blend the seam. Add a few complete flower and leaf elements to cover and conceal the cut through the design. Roll these elements into the background firmly with a small rod (**K**).

12 Roll the bead to smooth and refine the shape, keeping the needle in place. Trim the ends (**L**).

13 Bake the bead and then add a contrast to the ends to conceal the scrap clay core (**M**). After the second baking, sand and polish the entire bead.

A — 1" solid color.

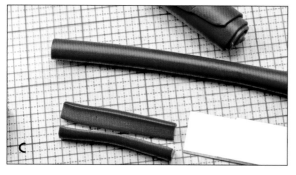

B

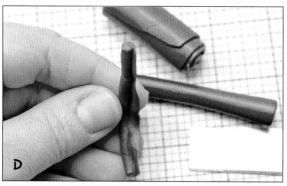

C

D

E

F

Rose

No floral shop is successful without the most popular flower—the rose. Let's wrap up our floral designs by exploring the American Beauty.

1 Roll a blended sheet from medium to dark red and make sure that there is a wide area of darker red at one end of the blend. The entire sheet should be at least 3x4 in. (**A**).

2 Thin the blended sheet and roll it into a spiral. Cut the spiral in half and reduce one piece to about 5 in. (**B**).

3 Cut off a 2-in. section. Reduce the cane more and cut off another 2-in. section. Repeat for another slightly thinner piece. Cut the thinnest cane lengthwise into two half-circles (**C**).

4 Begin with one half-circle piece and flatten it to make it wider. Roll it into a spiral with the darker red to the outside (**D**).

5 Flatten the other half-circle piece slightly and wrap it around the first spiral as a petal wraps around its center (**E**).

6 Divide the next larger cane in half lengthwise and add each half as slightly larger petals around the center with the dark edge to the outside (**F**).

7 Repeat with the third piece of the cane to make the fifth and sixth petals (**G**).

8 Repeat the process with the remaining section of the original blend until the rose has as many petals as desired and is as big as desired (**H**).

9 The end of the rose trimmed clean to show the image (**I**).

10 It is useful to reduce the size of a cane only on one end and preserve the original size on the other. This gives more design options later (**J**).

11 To make a set of beads for a necklace, use a black/pearl mix as a background color. Apply leaves and the small roses (**K**).

12 When rolling the cane slices into the background, be careful not to smear or distort the surface. Pierce the bead. It's ready to bake (**L**).

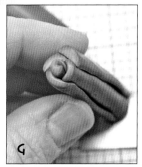
G

H

I

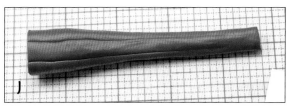
J

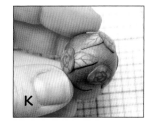
K

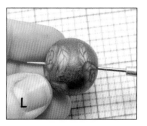
L

Bouquet

We've got a whole collection of flower canes. Let's be real floral designers and build a bouquet!

1 Begin with a subtly shaded background of minty and olive greens. Apply stems and leaves to begin a composition (**A**).

2 Next, add a few of each of the flowers and let them overlap each other. The morning glory is an accent flower, so reduce the cane until it is very small (**B**).

3 Roll smooth (**C**). Cut the desired shape, layer it on a background sheet, and bake to create an elegant pendant.

Translucent Canes and Overlay Patterns

The last collection of canes we will explore are designs that incorporate a large amount of translucent clay. When these colors and patterns are layered on a background, various elements will show through differently. The secrets to effectively layering translucent canes include incorporating fine lines in the canes, slicing canes as thin as possible, and keeping the surface as smooth as possible so the translucent cane elements won't be sanded off in the finishing stage.

Floating Geometrics

Let's begin with some simple geometric shapes that are filled with translucent clay. These elements will be layered and appear to float over a patterned background.

1 The first cane is a windowpane. Layer thin sheets of black between thick slabs of translucent (**A**).

2 Cut the block across the stripes into four pieces. Restack, with thin layers of black between each section and on the ends (**B**). Set aside.

3 Wrap a log of translucent with a neutral color. I used a coppery gold shade (**C**).

4 Make a spiral of translucent wrapped in a light olive color (**D**).

5 Look back through your collection of canes and select a simple pattern that has colors that coordinate with the translucent canes just made. Arrange a sheet of pattern from slices of this cane (**E**).

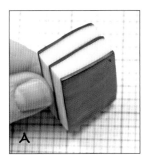

A

B

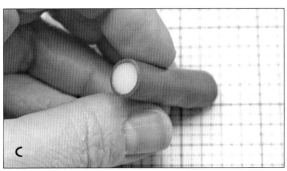

C

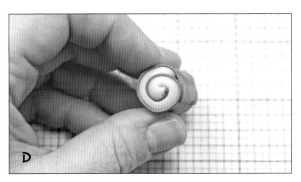

D

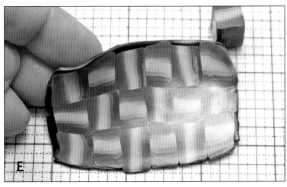

E

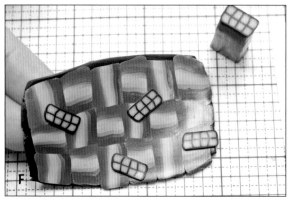

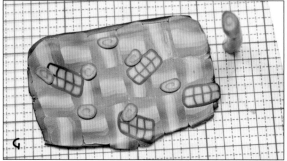

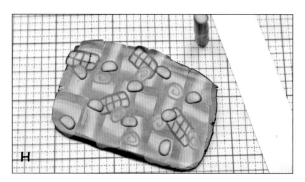

6 Begin applying very thin slices of the largest pattern. Roll the slices into the background with a small roller (**F**).

7 Scatter more slices of another pattern over the sheet. Overlap some of the elements (**G**).

8 Add the third pattern in thin slices, filling open spaces and completing the composition (**H**).

9 Roll the entire surface smooth (**I**).

10 Wrap around a pre-baked bead form. Be careful to blend the seams. If necessary, add a few more of the translucent elements to disguise the seams (**J**).

11 This is the baked but unsanded surface. Notice that the translucent areas are slightly clearer after baking (**K**).

12 Sanding and polishing also makes the translucent layer appear clearer as the smooth polished surface allows light to reflect off and refract through the surface better (**L**).

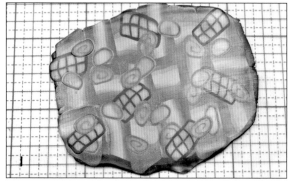

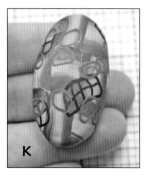

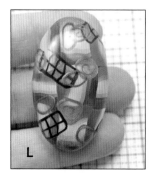

Line Drawing

Translucent canes can be simple forms, or they can be very elaborate and have subjective content. Next, let's try a cane that will contain a line drawing of a leaf.

1 Draw a simple pattern on a piece of card stock. This is going to be a ginkgo leaf which is one of my favorites (**A**).

2 Begin with a shaded cane for depth and variety in the line (**B**). The line will be light cream down the center and black on the edges. When reduced to be very thin, this will have a subtle effect.

3 Pinch and roll the color blend by hand until it is thin enough to go through the pasta machine (**C**).

4 Roll the color blend to a medium thickness (**D**). Use this for all the lines of the leaf.

5 The translucent clay leaf begins with a bit of detail, a row of dots (made from the blend created in step 4) that will lie inside the border (**E**).

6 Add a vein, again made from the blend created in step 4 (**F**).

7 Add the roundness of the center of the leaf with translucent clay, then wrap the entire shape with part of the sheet made in step 4 (**G**).

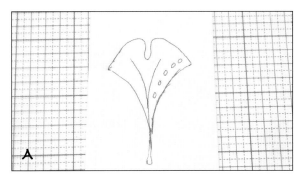

A

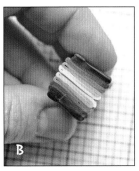

B

C

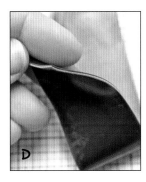

D

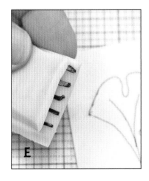

E

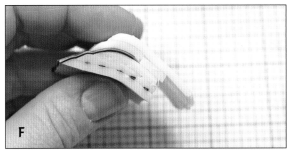

F

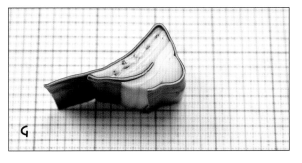

G

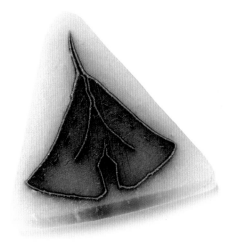

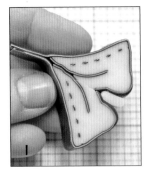

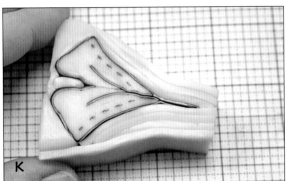

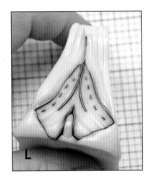

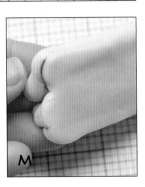

8 Divide the leaf cane in two (**H**).

9 Put the two halves together as shown. Add a snake of translucent between them to separate the lobes of the leaf in the center (**I**).

10 To reduce the leaf cane, encase the entire cane in more translucent clay until you create a manageable shape. Square up the end of the leaf (**J**).

11 Add more translucent along each side to form a rough triangle (**K**).

12 The cane is ready to be consolidated and reduced (**L**).

13 Translucent clay often has a different feel and firmness than pigmented clay. It is important to press and squeeze the length of the clay while reducing in order to minimize the distortion (**M**).

14 Here is the cane trimmed to reveal the undistorted image (**N**).

15 Use a marbled sheet of greens and golds to cover with the ginkgo leaf cane slices (**O**).

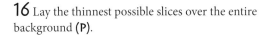

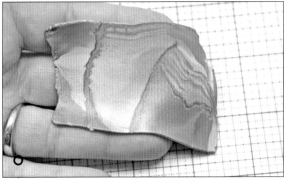

16 Lay the thinnest possible slices over the entire background (**P**).

17 Roll the surface smooth to seal the seams (**Q**). Cut any shape you desire.

18 Back the shape, and it's ready to bake. Note the color of the translucent and the background before baking (**R**).

19 Note the background showing through the much clearer translucent layer after baking, sanding, and polishing (**S**).

Here's another use of that ginkgo leaf on a bead.

20 Cover a base bead with slices of a cream-to-white spiral blend cane. Apply a layer of the translucent ginkgo over that (**T**).

21 Roll the bead to blend the seams, then flatten to make a large, flat focal bead (**U**).

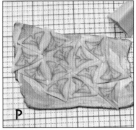

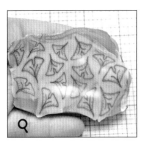

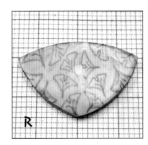

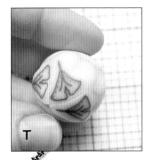

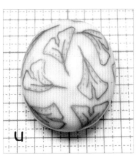

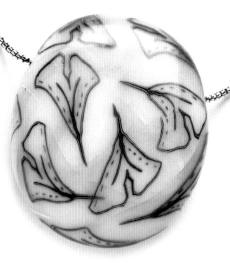

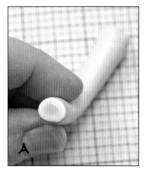

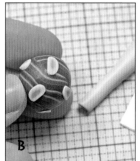

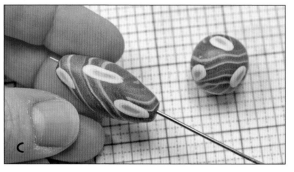

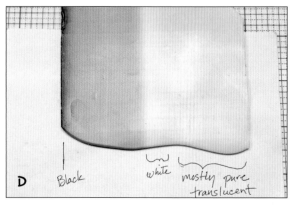

D — Black   white   mostly pure translucent

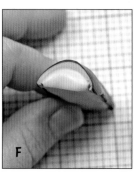

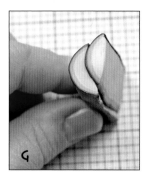

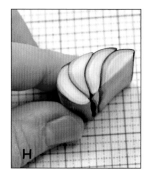

Translucent Color Blend

Since all of the cane styles we've explored have included a variation using blended colors, let's explore blending translucent and solid color in a Skinner blend for overlay canes.

1 Create a spiral cane with a blend between white and translucent (**A**).

2 Cover a core bead in slices of a stripe cane. Apply thin dots as well and roll in (**B**).

3 Reshape the beads into long bicones. See the color peeking through the center of the dots (**C**)?

I decided that this experiment worked well enough that I wanted to try again with a more complex cane. And I added a twist to the color blend.

1 Begin with a blend that flows from black to white and then into translucent (**D**). (See p. 18–19 for making a Skinner blend with more than two colors.)

2 Divide the blended sheet into two pieces. Stack one half of the blended sheet into a stripe cane from solid black on one side to translucent on the other (**E**).

3 Morph the cane from a block to a crescent, pulling the black side out and around (**F**).

4 Reduce and repeat the crescent. The beginning of a leaf shape is forming (**G**).

5 Add more crescents (**H**).

6 Roll the reserved piece of the blend (from step 2) into a spiral for the other side of the leaf (**I**).

7 Pinch the leaf into shape (**J**) ...

8 ... and add a stem (**K**).

9 Here is the leaf cane sliced thin and ready to apply to a background color (**L**).

10 As on p. 70, begin with a branch or vine and then apply the leaves (**M**).

11 A little contrast pattern adds a nice touch to the leaf design (**N**).

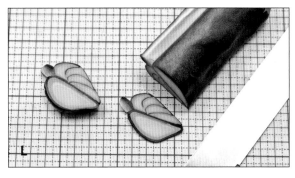

ARTIST'S GALLERY

An ikat cane built with several different color blends of blue, red and gold.

Collage pendant with several cane patterns, a texture layer, and a metal clay accent layer.

86

Focal pendant bead of a blend
of golds with floating solid and
translucent canes on top.

The black-and-white combination cane makes a sophisticated pair of earrings with hand-formed wires.

The distorted ends of a reduced cane on a background of black for a pop-art effect.

A reshaped shaded spiral cane forms the basis of this simple yet elegant brooch.

Another example of simplicity.

89

A collage pendant exploring the limits of coordinating colors, with metal clay on top.

These beads were created with leftovers from several early lessons in this book.

An organic repeat of a
bull's-eye cane.

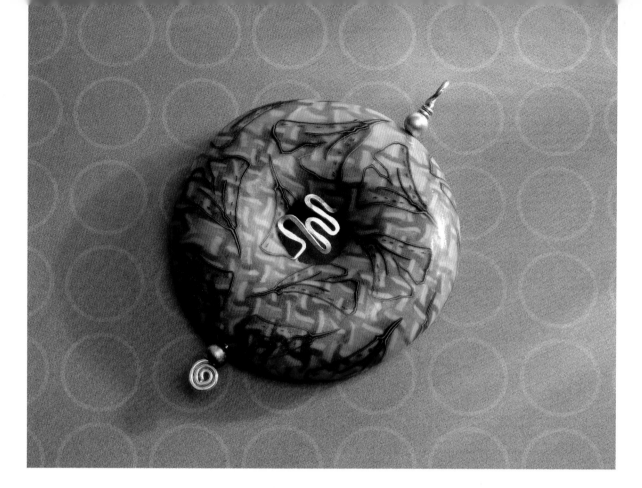

An exploration of translucent pattern over another pattern.

A simple pattern is made sophisticated with layering.

This set shows coordination in color along with contrasting ordered and organic patterns.

Acknowledgments

My sincerest thanks to my family for all the support and encouragement that went into this effort. They are my cheering section.

Throughout my art career, I have enjoyed the support of the good folks at Polyform Products Co., the makers of my favorite Premo Sculpey clays. They provided all the clay used in the projects in this book, and they generously support my teaching commitments as well.

Thanks also to Karin, my editor, and everyone at Kalmbach Books who make my designs and the books look so beautiful.

Finally, as J.S. Bach always penned at the bottom of his compositions:

Soli Deo Gloria—to God alone be the glory.

About the Author

Patricia Kimle has always been involved in art, from childhood on. Her early interests focused on apparel design and later, jewelry. Patricia holds a Ph.D. in textiles and clothing from Iowa State University. She taught apparel design courses at the college level for seven years.

Patricia has been exploring polymer clay for over 20 years. She is also a certified instructor for metal clay. She combines fine silver metal clay with polymer to create mixed-media jewelry. Patricia sells her jewelry to galleries and gift shops across the country. She has two lines: a fashion line, which combines silver and polymer with a strong nature theme, and an inspirational line, which incorporates scripture verses and prayers in the silver. She uses all original drawings, carved designs, and molds of foliage collected in her own yard in her artwork.

Patricia has written more than 30 project articles for jewelry and craft publications. Her first book, *Polymer Clay Inspirations,* was published in 2005. In 2010, her book *Perfectly Paired: Designing Jewelry with Polymer and Metal Clays* was published. She teaches polymer and metal clay at events around the country, including the Bead&Button Show.

Patricia lives on a small hobby farm in Ames, Iowa, with her husband and three children, a large garden, sheep, a few chickens, and a dog. She enjoys cooking and needle arts when she's not in the studio.

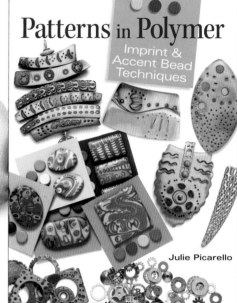